Landmark Visitors Guide

Isles of Mull,
Iona & Staffa

Hilary M. Peel

Published by

Landmark Publishing
Ashbourne Hall, Cokayne Ave, Ashbourne,
Derbyshire DE6 1EJ England

Published by:
Landmark Publishing Ltd,
Ashbourne Hall, Cokayne Avenue, Ashbourne, Derbyshire DE6 1EJ England
E-mail landmark@clara.net Web-site www.landmarkpublishing.co.uk

ISBN: 978-1-84306-439-8

© **Hilary M. Peel**

3rd Landmark edition 2009

British Library Cataloguing in Publication Data:
A catalogue record for this book is available from the British Library

Print: Gutenberg Press, Malta
Design & Cartography: Michelle Hunt

Front cover: Tobermory **Back cover top:** Iona Abbey
Back cover bottom-left: Benmore & Loch Scridain, Mull **bottom-right:** Staffa

Photograph credits:
Stephen Hopkins; 15 top-right, 34, 35t, 35b, 39b, 43, 51, 54, 63, 76 **W. H. Clegg;** 15 top-left
and middle, 26b, 27, 46t **Mark Titterton;** 46b, 74, 82, 86, 71t **Christopher Coates;** 47
VisitScotland; back cover bottom-left & right, 6, 7,14t, 14b, 15b, 26t, 30-1b, 50, 55, 59b
Phil McDermott Photography; 38 & 42

Shutterstock with copyright to:
Stephen Finn; 7 **Mary Lane;** 11 **Bill McKelvie;** back cover top & 75 large

All other photography by Lindsey Porter

About This Guide
This guide book is meant merely to whet your appetite. It is not an exhaustive work – a
large tome would be needed for that and, indeed, there are many books about aspects
of these islands, some of which are listed at the end. The tours in each chapter can,
of course, be done in either direction or can be joined at any point. Several days may
be needed to do justice to some of them. Exploring by foot off the roads is wonderfully
rewarding but please treat the countryside with respect and take sensible precautions
wherever you go.

While every care has been taken to ensure that the information in this guide is as accurate
as possible at the time of publication, the publisher and author accept no responsibility
for any loss, injury or inconvenience sustained by anyone using this book. Please note
that places of interest etc are indicated on the maps to help you plan your trip but it is
recommended to have a large scale map when walking or touring by car.

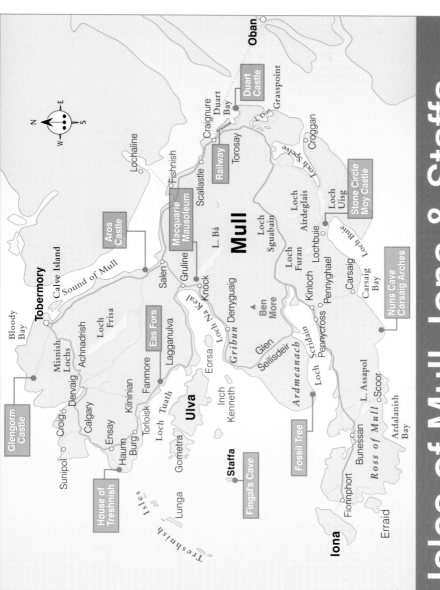

Isles of Mull, Iona & Staffa

Contents

WELCOME TO THE ISLES OF MULL, IONA & STAFFA   **6**

The Island of Mull   6
Spelling and pronunciation   7
Geology   8
Archaeology   9
Map: Tobermory   10
History   10
    The clan wars   10
    Famine and the clearances   10
Natural history   13
    Climate   16
Marine Archaeology   16
Food & Drink   17

1. THE NORTH OF MULL   **18**

Tobermory   18
History   19
    Around Town   20
    World War II   21
    Balamory   22
Walk1 Upper Town   21
Walk 2 Aros Park   23
A drive or walk round the top
    of the town   23
Walk 3 To the Lighthouse   25
Glengorm   25
Walk to Dun Ara   27
Walk inland past An Sean Dun   27
Walk to ruined villages and
    the coast   28
Tobermory to Dervaig   28
On to Calgary   29
Moorlands and ruined villages   31
    Walk to the Whisky Cave   32

Loch Tuath   32
Loch na Keal to Aros   36
Aros Castle   37

2. CENTRAL MULL - SALEN TO CROGGAN   **38**

Craignure   41
Torosay   44
Duart   44
Lochdonhead   45
Loch Spelve   45
Rare Stone Circle   46
Lochbuie   47
Moy Castle   47
Walk 1 Lochbuie to Carsaig   48
Walk 2 Lochbuie to Glenmore   48
Croggan   49

3. CENTRAL MULL - GLEN MORE TO GRULINE   **50**

Ardmeanach   52
Gribun   53
    Ben More   54
    Walk along Loch Ba   55
Gruline   57

4. BROLAS AND THE ROSS OF MULL   **58**

Kinloch   58
Carsaig   58
    Walks at Carsaig   59
Scoor   60
Bunessan   61

Fionnphort 61
   Kintra 62

5. OFF SHORE ISLANDS 63
History of the islands 63
Ulva and Gometra 63
Ulva 65
Inch Kenneth 65
   History 66
Treshnish Islands 67
Erraid 68

6. IONA 70
Book of Kells 72
History 73
Around the Abbey 74
   The High Crosses 75
   Within the Abbey 76
   The Nunnery 77
   The Iona Community 77
The north end of Iona 78
Central Iona 80
The south end of Iona 81

7. STAFFA 82
Geology 82
Early visitors 82
History 83
Ownership of Staffa 84
Visiting the island 85

FACTFILE 88
Travelling to Mull 88
Accommodation 88
Air Field 88

Banks 89
Boat hire 89
Angling 89
Whale watching 89
Books 90
Churches 90
Diving 91
Emergencies 91
Events 91
Fishing 91
Food, drink & crafts 91
Garages 92
Getting around 93
Public Transport 93
Golf 94
Medical information 94
Local Papers 94
Maps 94
Photography 94
Pony Trekking 94
Post offices 94
Tourist information & online sites 95
Veterinary surgeon 95
Visitor attractions & Activities 95

Feature Boxes

Top Tips 7
Balamory 22
Whisky 24
Aros Castle 37
Glemore Stories 56
Book of Kells 71
St Columba 72
Within the Abbey
  of St Columba 76

Welcome to the
Isles of Mull, Iona & Staffa

The Island of Mull

Travelling to Mull is easier than many people think. Oban to Craignure is the main route from the mainland but ferries also cross from Lochaline in Morvern to Fishnish, and Kilchoan in Ardnamurchan to Tobermory. Coming via Oban means that you could use train or bus from your starting point, but the other two ferry points are most easily reached by car, motorbike or bicycle. Private planes can land on Mull at the Glenforsa air strip.

In summer the ferries are frequent but, in winter especially, check what time they run. It is always best to book your vehicle with Caledonian MacBrayne on the Craignure route. For information to help you plan your journey, see the Factfile.

Arriving on Mull you leave the hustle and bustle of the mainland behind. Sometimes it takes a while to adjust to the change of pace, to use senses that may have become unresponsive, like under-used muscles, but before long you will relax and become aware of the sights and sounds around you.

Most of the roads on Mull are single track. This means that one must drive with care and courtesy. Leave plenty of time for your journeys and remember that the black and white poles mark passing places, not parking places! Always remain on the left-hand side of the road, even if the passing place is on the opposite side, just stop level with it and let the on-coming car go in to pass you. Nasty accidents can happen if you suddenly swerve across in front of the other vehicle. Passing places are also there to allow following traffic to overtake you as you may wish to make a more leisurely journey. As you pass you may get a friendly wave, especially if you have been kind enough to back instead of trying to squeeze past on the verge where there may be a hidden ditch or drainage channel!

Spelling and pronunciation

The spelling of Gaelic place names quite often varies a little and even Gaelic speakers are not always agreed. Surnames have sometimes been spelled differently over the years and it is only comparatively recently that they have

Top Tips

- Duart Castle

- Torosay Castle and Gardens

- Little Railway at Craignure

- Tobermory (Balamory) - many attractions

- Whale Watching & Sea Life trips

- Sea eagle viewing at Loch Frisa

- Organised Wild Life trips by minibuses

- Kilmore Church at Dervaig

- Ulva Island

- Puffins etc on the Treshnish Islands

- Iona Abbey and Island

Top: Duart Castle
Bottom: Iona

become standardized. For instance, at one time Mac, Mc or, even, M' were used by the same person as the fancy took him! The pronunciation of Gaelic is difficult for the non–speaker, but some indication of the most usual way has been given for the places mentioned in this text.

Geology

Any visitor to Mull, Iona and Staffa must be impressed by the variety of scenery which these islands represent. Mull with its mountains, some having a distinctive staircase-like silhouette, its soaring cliffs and red granite, its caves and coves and moorland; Iona with its glittering sandy bays, grass thick with flowers and marble; Staffa with its immense columns and Fingal's cave. Just as skeletons give distinctive shapes to the human body, so the underlying geology of these three islands have resulted in their very different outward appearances.

Billions of years ago Scotland and England were not joined. They were just two of the 'plates' that drifted all round the world becoming tropical deserts, swamps or ice fields according to their latitude. It is only about 400 million years since they collided and, for several millions years after this, the join, roughly where Hadrian's wall stands, continued to suffer stress and strain as the land masses ground against each other. Huge mountains were thrust up, chains of enormous volcanoes continually erupted and gigantic glaciers and walls of ice appeared and disappeared.

Some of the oldest rocks in Scotland, if not the world, are to be found on Iona. They were formed before the collision, about 2,500 to 3,000 million years ago. Compared to these, the gigantic volcanoes that exploded on Mull after England and Scotland had met, were newcomers. It is their much eroded roots which can still be seen and the resultant outpouring of molten lava from these and subsequent explosions produced a plateau thousands of feet thick, layer upon layer, stretching far out into the Atlantic, even as far as Europe and Iceland. Earthquakes shattered the layers, storms of unbelievable ferocity carved through them and ice, higher than Ben Nevis, formed on top. The stupendous weight of the ice depressed the land, glaciers and frosts sculpted it, scouring out glens and leaving behind moraines and erratics. Several times the sea level rose and fell as ice melted and re-formed, resulting in raised beaches. Some of the best examples of these can be seen looking across Loch Scridan towards Burg from Bunessan, in the Ross of Mull.

Geologists came from far and wide to see the two caldera, the ring dyke at Loch Ba and the trap scenery of Ardmeanach, to search for fossils and McCulloch's 60 million year old fossilised tree on Burg. There are semi-precious stones to be found, the ancient leaf beds of Ardtun, basalt columns, pillow lavas, granites and sandstone. There are even a few seams of lignite on Mull and on Iona there is marble. For the layman, and for children too, these islands are wonderful hunting grounds, especially in the Ross of Mull and on Iona where beautiful pebbles and shells can be found.

Archaeology

Evidence of man's occupation in these islands goes back about 6,000 years. A few stone and bone tools, and numbers of flint implements have been found which indicate that late Mesolithic man probably came to the islands. It is possible that these nomadic people, who lived by hunting, fishing and gathering plants, may have occupied some of the caves in the Ross of Mull.

By the Neolithic period some farming groups appear to have been established, judging from the evidence of chambered burial cairns and fragments of pottery which have been found. These people lived in communities and made themselves much more permanent and relatively comfortable dwellings. None has survived on these islands but there are Neolithic cairns, usually sited near land that was suitable for cultivation and within reach of small bays.

The Bronze Age emerged gradually from the Neolithic period and, by about 2,500 BC amazing structures began to appear. These were the standing stones and stone circles, which in their day and age, were comparable with the great cathedrals of over 3000 years later. Mull is especially rich in standing stones, having at least 24 separate sites, which range from individual monoliths to alignments of several stones. The best example of a stone circle is at Lochbuie. The purpose of these silent relics of long ago is a matter of fierce debate but they seem to have had some ceremonial purpose and often to have been associated with burials. In addition many seem to be connected with the movements of the sun, moon and stars. Whatever their purpose they were astonishing constructions which must have involved an enormous expenditure of time, effort and manpower as well as a high degree of engineering skill.

The late Bronze Age, moving into the Iron Age, was the period in which many of the forts, duns and brochs were built. Duns were fairly small defensive structures with one thick dry-stone wall, whilst brochs were round towers with double walls in which there were stairs leading to small rooms. They were practically impregnable and, inside was space for the animals which had become increasingly important to the way of life. There are nearly 60 duns, forts and brochs on the islands as well as six crannogs – dwellings on artificial islands created in inland lochs and often linked to the shore by a causeway. Again, the construction of these, in days long before mechanical assistance, must have required a vast use of available resources.

Much has been written about the early Christian era. Probably by the fifth or sixth century AD a Gaelic speaking people known as the Dal Riata had colonized the Inner Hebrides and adjacent mainland and their kingdom was called Dalraida. It was the king of Dalraida who gave Columba the island of Iona where he founded his monastery.

The next 400 or so years do not seem to have left much evidence behind them on the islands but from the mediaeval period – 12th to 16th centuries – there is much that has survived, particularly in the shape of ruined chapels and castles. Man's occupation of the last 400 years is, of course, clearly seen through the ruins of cottages and villages and marks

Origin of 'Hebrides'

By the first century AD this group of islands, north of Ireland, had become known as far afield as Greece. Here they were called the Ebudes, which became Hebudes and, eventually, Hebrides.

in the landscape indicating his farming activities.

History

After the time of the Picts, Scots, Angles, Celts and others who invaded the north of Britain, the Western and Northern Isles became subject to Norway until Somerled emerged as a leader in the 12th century. When he was killed in 1164 one of his sons, Dugald, took possession of Lorne and Mull.

Until the late 13th century much of the Inner Hebrides remained in the possession of the MacDougalls of Lorne. But, during the wars of this period, they were defeated by Macdonalds who then took the title 'Lords of the Isles'. One of the Macdonald daughters married a Maclean chief in 1367 and, as a dowry she brought land on Mull to the Macleans. In 1493, after 140 years the Lordship of the Isles ceased to exist and all the lands that they owned were surrendered to James IV, who distributed much of it amongst his allies – the powerful men of the time.

The clan wars

The 16th century has been called an age of turbulence and James V, not long before he died, visited his quarrelsome and rebellious island chiefs in order to subdue them. In 1540 he took back much of their lands and granted a charter to the Macleans of Duart, who thus came into possession of

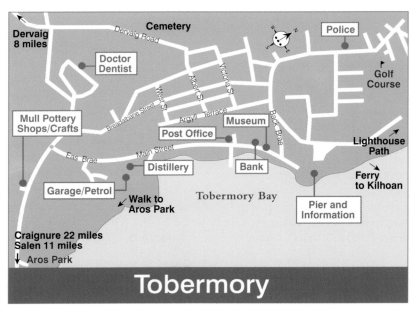

Tobermory

The remains of a crofter's cottage

more than half of Mull. Amongst other people who owned smaller areas of the islands at this time were MacKinnons, MacQuarries and two other Maclean clans – one of Coll and the other of Lochbuie.

By the time of James VI of Scotland, the Macleans of Duart had fought so many wars and mismanaged their affairs so badly that they had accumulated large debts. The Campbell Earls of Argyll stepped in to take these over, on security of Maclean lands and possessions. Eventually this paid a great part in the downfall of the Macleans of Duart.

Ferocious battles continued, both between Scotland and England and between clans. The Campbells of Argyll were particularly ambitious and they found the Macleans stood in their way time after time. In 1647 there was an especially bloody confrontation, which

resulted in Duart Castle being surrendered to the Campbells. But worse was to follow when, in 1651 hundreds of Mull men were slaughtered at the battle of Inverkeithing. A series of bad winters and harvests leading to famine, disease and death did nothing to help the remaining population.

In 1674 the feud between the Macleans and Campbells culminated in an invasion of Mull by government troops and Campbells, who perpetrated cruelties on the ordinary people that resulted in the Macleans finally having to capitulate five years later. For over 200 years the Macleans of Duart, who had been so prominent in the early years, played little part in the history of the islands and their great castle gradually fell into ruin.

So, at the start of the 18th century the three islands were mostly owned by Campbells of Argyll and Macleans of

Conducting clan business in the 16th century

Traditionally at this time, land was mostly held by tacksmen or middle men, usually relatives of the clan chief, who, in their turn, sublet to tenants. Rents had to be paid not only in money but also in produce such as butter, corn, eggs or in animals or in military service. Such a chain of subletting, combined with the poverty of the crofters, often resulted in rents being late or not being paid at all. Add to this the continual expense of fighting wars and keeping up appearances in terms of castles, galleys and retinues of servants, and it is no wonder that the purse of many a clan was stretched to breaking point.

Lochbuie. (It was not until the middle of the 20th century that the Lochbuie family began to spell their name Maclaine.) The Campbells rarely came to their property and it brought in very little income. The battle of Culloden in 1746, at which the Jacobites were defeated by government forces under the Duke of Cumberland, seemed to mark the point at which the clan system finally collapsed. 'Butcher' Cumberland and his troops committed vicious atrocities and a series of statutes, depriving the chiefs of their land and their traditions, caused deep despair and loss of heart. Clan feuds dwindled and the Highlands gradually succumbed to the rule of law.

Famine and the clearances

As the personalities of successive generations of Campbells and Macleans changed, so the old passions died. By the late 18th century, the Campbell lands were being looked after by a series of factors, some of whom were good and some cruel, but it was not until the early 19th century that a Duke of Argyll himself came to visit his property. As had many before him, he found himself short of money, an affliction of later Dukes and many of their fellow landowners.

Estates began to be broken up and to change hands during the early to mid-19th century. New men appeared on the scene who did not have any feelings of responsibility for the tenants whom they found living on their land. Some of these tenants were lucky but many were not. Kelp manufacture provided an income for a while but the end of the Napoleonic wars dealt a mortal blow to this and, at the same time, the price of cattle and herring dropped disastrously. The final straw came with the potato blights of the 1840s. Potato was such a staple crop that families literally starved when this failed. Poverty and malnutrition stalked the islands.

In the middle of the 19th century the population of the islands was over 10,000. By the end of the century it had gone down dramatically. It is tempting to put this all down to the 'clearances' by cruel and greedy landlords. In parts of Mull this was undoubtedly the case, especially in the Ross, but in other areas it was not so. The social historian must examine the whole of this, and preceding centuries, very carefully before coming to conclusions that might be too generalized and sweeping. However, it is certain that many people suffered great hardship and were forced, for one reason or another, to leave their homes.

The late 19th century saw the start of a slightly happier time for some families as the fashion for visiting the Highlands and buying estates meant that jobs were available either on the estates or in the big houses. It was also possible for the young to go away, if they wanted, to seek work in towns and cities further south. Improved means of transport and communication gradually helped link the island communities to the wider world.

Natural history

Of all the Hebridean islands it is probably true that Mull, Iona and Staffa cover the greatest variety of scenery. Between them they have sea cliffs, rocky and sandy beaches, farming land, coniferous and deciduous woodland, open moors, freshwater lochs and mountains. Their underlying rocks and resultant soil structure produce conditions in which a profusion of plants, trees, rushes, sedges, mosses and lichens flourish. These, in turn, provide a diversity of habitats, which are rich in insects, crustaceans, fish, birds and animals – truly, a paradise for the naturalist whether professional or amateur, young or old.

On Mull and Iona, much of this abundant natural history is easily accessible. Even from the roads, for those who cannot walk far, patient observers will find much of interest, especially if they possess a keen eye and a pair of binoculars. There are also guided walks and organized wild life tours either by boat or by land rover.

Visitors are usually anxious to spot a red deer, an otter, eagle or whale. Admittedly these are wonderful to see but there are many more sightings to be made of less spectacular, but maybe rarer, species. There are fallow deer on Mull and one or two of them have white coats. Mountain hare, polecat and, unfortunately, mink can often be seen – but there are no foxes. On a boat trip you might spot dolphins of several types, minke whales and even a basking shark, whilst seals are common and often sun themselves on skerries just off the land, looking like slugs or upturned bananas! Seals are innately nosy creatures and will frequently poke their heads out of the water to watch you!

The Forestry Commission own many acres on Mull and their plantations, of sitka, Norway spruce and larch, nowadays include broadleaved trees, which has had a beneficial effect upon wild life. Within the hushed, close-packed woods are mosses, lichens, fungi and insects, as well as the bird life.

Between two and three hundred species of birds have been recorded on the islands, some merely passing through, some migrants and some resident all the year. From the tiny goldcrest to the enormous sea eagle, the comical puffin to the solemn grey heron, the shy and scarce ptarmigan to the ubiquitous oyster catcher, the silent short-eared owl to the garrulous gull, bird watchers can be sure of year round interest.

In winter, of course, not many flowers

Staffa

Asknish Bay

Above left: Spotted orchid
Above right: Fragrant orchid

Puffin on Lunga

The beauty of Mull

Mull has been likened to an opal – unexpected changes of light and angle bring out hitherto unseen shades and depths. Wherever you go the scenery alters as you round the next bend in the road, as the sun suddenly blazes forth or as the time of day changes. Naturally, it is better if the sun shines but even in bad weather there is mystery in the cloud shrouded mountains, fierce power in the sight of waterfalls being blown upwards so that the hills seem to be on fire and soothing harmony in the wind rippled grass, the drifting clouds and birds soaring with outstretched wings.

Loch Assapol

are to be found. But those who venture at this time of year will be rewarded with a feast of colour from a different source as seaweed, lichen and bare twigs contrast with the pale, dead grasses, sometimes being illuminated into vivid life by a glorious winter sun. Then, as spring arrives, the cliffs and road sides become covered with the delicate, pale blooms of hundreds of primroses interspersed with the golden glow of celandine. From then on the botanist, or just the wild flower lover, will never regret having come to the islands. Orchids, sundew, butterwort, cotton grass, dog violets, lousewort, the list is endless with, naturally, bell heather, ling and cross-leaved heath to add autumn shades to the delicate grass of Parnassus and fairy flax. Expert and amateur alike cannot fail to be charmed.

Climate

It is as well to remember that the climate of these islands is extremely variable and unpredictable. Quite often it can be raining in one area and fine only a short distance away, so never despair! On the whole, the Ross of Mull and Iona have less rain than the northern part of Mull. Because of the warm North Atlantic Drift the winters are rarely very cold but, of course, there is snow on the hills and mountains. Anyone who goes walking off the roads, at any time of year, should take sensible precautions because, even on a summer's day, the weather may change rapidly and low cloud or mist can be disorientating. Always inform someone where you are going and take extra clothing, food, stout shoes and, if possible, a mobile phone.

It is important to respect the land, the plants and the animals. It is not true to say that there is no law of trespass in Scotland; most of it is owned by someone and, frequently, it is farming land where sheep or cattle roam. Dogs must always be under control and, especially in spring, they must be on a lead. In autumn great care is needed on the hills because of the shooting season. Try to move quietly and never go too close to a bird's nest, or pick wild flowers. The true naturalist will always act with care and consideration, quietly observing, listening, sketching, learning and enjoying all that the islands have to offer.

Marine Archaeology

Mull and its surrounding islands lie in dangerous waters. Their coastlines are rocky and the seas around teem with skerries (reefs), submerged rocks and small islets, added to which are the currents, tides and sudden unexpected squalls. Sailors of all sizes of craft, from a canoe up to the big ferries, must take every precaution. Over the centuries there have been dozens of shipwrecks in the area and divers from far and near come to explore them. As such people know, each of the wrecks is a memorial to the men and women who died in them and must be treated with care and respect.

Some of the wrecks around Mull are protected sites and two of these are *HMS Dartmouth* and *The Swan*. The former was a wooden warship in the service of the crown during the Jacobite troubles in the highlands. It had been sent to force the Maclean of

Duart chief to swear allegiance to the crown but it encountered a violent storm that swept it from its shelter in Scallastle Bay. There were only six survivors from the 130 or so on board. *The Swan* was a Cromwellian ship which sank just off Duart Point in 1653. The watchers on the shore could see and hear the victims but could not save them. Details of this wreck are to be found in Duart Castle.

In 1918 the *Aurania* was torpedoed out in the Atlantic and the rope broke as she was being towed to the Clyde. She drifted on to Caillach Point on Mull where she broke up. The aptly, but sadly, named *Mountaineer* ran aground on Lady Rock in 1889. There was no loss of life as she balanced long enough for all the passengers to be rescued. A trawler called the *Robert Limbrick* was smashed on Quinish Point by hurricane force winds. None of her crew survived.

The *Maine*, carrying wounded men, was wrecked in 1914 in dense fog off the south coast of Mull. Whilst waiting for rescue the hospital cases aboard were taken on shore and tents were erected to house them. All but the captain of the *Hispania* were saved when she sank in the Sound of Mull in 1954. This is one of the most scenic wrecks in Scotland. These are but a few of the wrecks around these coasts that attract many divers year after year.

This guide book is meant merely to whet your appetite. It is not an exhaustive work – a large tome would be needed for that and, indeed, there are many books about aspects of these islands, some of which are listed at the end. The tours in each chapter can, of course, be done in either direction or can be joined at any point. Several days may be needed to do justice to some of them. Exploring by foot off the roads is wonderfully rewarding but please treat the countryside with respect and take sensible precautions wherever you go.

Local Food and Drink

On Mull and Iona can be found a wealth of local, organic food and drink. In fact, there is so much to choose from that each year, there is a week long Food Festival. It is usually held in the 3rd week of September. All over the islands events are planned where local produce is served – lamb, pork, beef, venison, haggis, shellfish, oysters, cheese, vegetables, mushrooms, clootie dumpling, shortbread, biscuits, honey, whisky – the list goes on and on. Many shops sell, and tearooms/restaurants serve, locally baked cakes, scones, oatcakes, pancakes and pastries. The Scottish are justly famous for their delicious home-baking which can often be enjoyed at ceilidhs and meetings of the numerous clubs and societies.

Organised by the Mull & Iona Community Trust, The Taste of Mull & Iona Food Festival promotes local food & produce. It retains a strong community identity of which the islanders are very proud. For further information, contact the Tourist Information Centre on 01680 812377.

Farmer's Markets are held in village halls in Dervaig, Craignure, Tobermory and Fionnphort. Look out for posters in the local shops.

Tobermory

The town of Tobermory is sometimes called the capital of Mull. Lying in the north-east of the island, its distinctively painted buildings are strung round a horseshoe shaped, sheltered bay like jewels on a bracelet.

In summer it is a bustling place, its one street thronged with people and cars and with many yachts and maybe a cruise liner anchored off-shore. This is the main shopping place for the island. Amongst the shops are a baker, fishmonger, butcher (now community owned and stocking local meat), a long established ironmonger and wine mer-chant, a Co-op and pharmacy. There is a hairdresser, small laundry and chandlery, as well as a branch of the Clydesdale Bank, Post Office and Youth Hostel. Craft shops, a silversmith, book shop and clothes shops can also be found.

Here you can book for any of the Caledonian MacBrayne ferries, book tickets for the theatre which is on the island, find information at the Tourist Office, fill up with petrol or have your car repaired. There are several hotels and restaurants, as well as places for bar meals and a Balti House. Chocoholics must not miss the handmade chocolate shop where the mere smell is enough to drive one crazy! It is also one of the places to come if you wish to book a sea trip, go fishing or view marine life

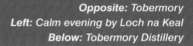

– the Hebridean Whale and Dolphin Trust have a base here which, though small, is packed with information. It has truly been said that in one relatively short street, Tobermory can cater for most things.

But there is much more that is of interest in Tobermory. The name – Tobar Mhoire – means the Well of Mary. No-one is sure which Mary this refers to but the footings of the medieval St Mary's Chapel can still be found inside the cemetery gates up the hill at the back of the town.

History

In the mid-18th century Tobermory Bay was used as an anchorage by Government ships which had been sent to search for Bonnie Prince Charlie. Some 20 years later Dr Samuel Johnson and Mr James Boswell landed on their tour of the Highlands. They thought it a fine port, full of sailing ships and were given a meal in a 'tolerable inn' by the shore. This can still be seen behind the Anchorage restaurant. The pair stayed the night in 'a strange confused house' which was Erray Farm House some distance up the hill and which now forms an outbuilding to the present house.

Until this time Tobermory had remained a small collection of cottages, no more important than anywhere else on Mull. Then, in 1788, the Duke of Argyll who owned the village, persuaded the British Society for Encouraging Fishing to develop it as a fishing station. Some of the first of the new buildings

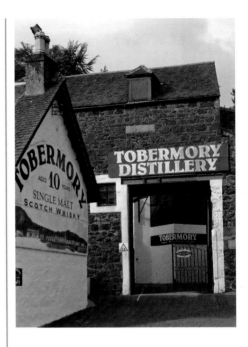

that were then erected are still in use. For instance, the present Post Office was the Customs House, where tax had to be paid on salt needed for the herring, and part of what is now the Co-op was an Inn. A little later a breast wall was built which reclaimed some 35 yards (32m) of land from the sea. Sadly, the project of turning Tobermory into a focus for the fishing industry failed in a very few years. The families who moved into the newly built upper town, rising on terraces up the steep hillside, were an agricultural people who found it impossible to change themselves into commercial fishermen. In any case, they were too far from the fishing grounds and from mainland outlets.

During the early to mid-19th century the town spread eastwards as people evicted from other parts of the island flooded in. This influx of the dispossessed made it into a poor area, especially as a combination of potato blight, hard winters and disease struck the population. However, as the Victorian age wore on, a new enthusiasm for tourism and travel was born and this saved the town. Distinguished visitors came, including Scott, Mendelssohn, Gladstone and Queen Victoria herself, and a deep-water pier was built. This, combined with the sheltered anchorage meant that it was easy to land people and goods safely. Wealthy men from the south bought Highland estates and Tobermory began to flourish. By 1875 it had become a burgh with a Provost. It remained thus for 100 years, perhaps the smallest burgh in Scotland.

Around the town

One of the buildings that cannot fail to be seen is on the top of the hill at the north side of the bay. This is the **Western Isles Hotel**. It was built in 1883 and was described as being a handsome building in an elevated site with 30 bedrooms, stables, a coach house, granary, harness room and a lawn tennis court. But, only 17 or 18 years later, it had to close and it did not reopen for over 30 years. It has been extended and has undergone many changes since then and is now a first class hotel with magnificent views.

Another distinctive feature of the town is the clock tower in the main street opposite the Co-op. This was erected in the early 1900s by Isabella Bird, one of the great lady travellers of the Victorian era, as a memorial to her sister, Henrietta. The sisters had a cottage near the Western Isles Hotel, which is still there, and came frequently. Isabella travelled all over the world during the last three decades of the 19th century. She went to the Rockies, Persia, Japan, Hawaii, Australia, Korea and Tibet, to name but a few. She climbed mountains, lived rough and travelled on foot, by pony, camel or whatever offered. Throughout her travels she wrote long letters to her sister, which formed the basis for her many books. Henrietta died of typhoid in 1880 and Isabella, who married a Dr Bishop shortly afterwards, paid for this memorial. It was designed by Charles, the brother of the mountaineer Edward Whymper, and is based upon a clock in Houghton, Huntingdonshire, which was where the sisters were born.

Nestling in the shadow of the clock you may miss a small **ornamental fountain**. A scantily dressed but charming female cherub balances precariously on a sausage shaped object whilst clutching an over sized bat! This may be an unfair description for the effect is delightful and she has maintained her position for over 120 years! Inscribed on the 'bat' is the record of its presentation in 1883 by the civil engineer who installed the new water supply for the town. He expressed the hope that the fountain would be useful to the inhabitants and to the many visitors who, he felt sure, would flock to the town in years to come.

Near to the Clydesdale Bank is the **Mull and Iona Museum**. This is run entirely by volunteers and is well worth a visit. It is amazing how much information can be found here, both downstairs and, for those who pay a small fee, in the upper library. Knowledgeable and helpful folk are on hand to help with queries if they can.

World War II

Tobermory is a busy, lively place and yet has an air of tranquillity. It was not always so. From 1940 until 1945 the bay and town were the headquarters of the Western Approaches Command. During these five years well over 1,000 small ships passed through, spending about 14 days in the bay under the command of Sir Gilbert Stephenson. It was his job to turn raw recruits, some scarcely out of school, into fighting crews able to cope with naval warfare. From Tobermory these ships went out to fight the 'Battle of the Atlantic', escorting convoys and hunting predatory U-boats. The man who achieved this transformation was nicknamed the 'Terror of Tobermory', feared but also loved and admired by the thousands of men, and some women, who passed through his hands. The inhabitants of the town became used to the mock exercises, sometimes involving explosions, which disturbed their peace, and the streets, churches and shops were filled with uniformed men and women.

Walk1 Upper Town

Between the Co-op and the Post Office is a steep zigzag path. Take it slowly – there is a rail and also a seat halfway up! Straight ahead at the top is the old school with, on its left, the **Parish Church**. Across the road to the right are the buildings of the present Tobermory school. The old school building has been turned into **An Tobar an Arts Centre and Gallery** where

Spanish treasure

Many people will have heard about the Spanish 'treasure ship' which is said to have sunk in Tobermory bay. For years it was thought to have been the *Florida* but, in fact, it was a Ragusan carrack from Dubrovnik called *San Juan de Sicilia* which had been commandeered by the Spaniards for use in their Armada fleet. By August 1588 the Spaniards had been defeated and their ships scattered by gales. The *San Juan* was forced to shelter in Tobermory bay. She was not a gold-laden pay ship but was, nevertheless, exotic and interesting. There are many stories about how she came to explode. One says that Maclean of Duart used some of the Spaniards aboard her to help in one of his battles against the MacDonalds and, when the captain of the *San Juan* recalled his men before Maclean had finished with them, the angry Chief demanded compensation. This being refused, a member of the Maclean clan hid on board and blew the ship up. There are other ideas but what is certain is that in November 1588 the *San Juan* blew apart and sank. Since then attempts have been made to find her and artefacts have been recovered – cannon, guns, an anchor, coins, plate, iron balls, pewter candlesticks – but no gold! The last salvage operations were in 1982.

Balamory

Tobermory, with its beautiful position and multi-coloured houses, became the setting for the popular children's television series Balamory. In the summer, especially, many families bring their young children to see the houses of some of the characters – Spencer the painter, Miss Hoolie, P.C. Plum and Suzi's Sweet Shop, for instance. It may be as well to warn your children that they will not see the Nursery School as these scenes were shot in the studios in Glasgow. Nor will they find Archie, the Inventor's, castle because this is in North Berwick. The railway on which the Balamory Express runs is not actually in Tobermory. It can be found at Craignure, where the ferry docks, but it is a walk of half a mile to the start of the train journey and it finishes at Torosay Castle where there is another shorter walk up to the tearoom, gardens and castle. Be warned that the colour of the train is not pink!

Shops in Tobermory sell many Balamory items – clothing, books, badges, mugs and so on. There is a Children's Animal Farm just outside Tobermory (☎ 07789 807910 www.tobermorychildrensfarm.co.uk) where there are young animals for children to enjoy and a tearoom to relax in.

'Mull & Iona Taxis' provide a tour to Tobermory to see the coloured houses and then to Torosay Castle or the Children's Farm or Duart Castle, finishing with a ride on the Balamory Express back to Craignure. Booking is essential. ☎ 07887 774550 or 01681 700507.

For more details of Balamory see www.tobermory.co.uk/balamory.

exhibitions and lectures are held and where home baking and, often, an open fire can be enjoyed. Turn left along the road below An Tobar and the church and go up to the latter. Before you actually enter stand outside to admire the view. From here the semi-circular bay seems almost blocked by the privately owned **Calve Island**, which has one house on it. To its right, on Mull, is a bright patch of green on a wooded hill. This is where **Aros House** stood until it was demolished in 1960. Behind you is the church, which was built in 1898 and is plain inside apart from an attractive rose window.

Return to the road you came along and continue to the right – **Argyll Terrace**. These houses, mostly rebuilt in the 19th century on the site of the original 18th century cottages, have attractive gardens across the terrace. Look at the view again as you walk. Cross Albert Street and continue on a narrower road that then becomes a footpath. Notice **Rhona Cottage** which used to be the prison and, hidden in the trees above it, is the present day Council Office building which housed malefactors when the old prison was closed. The path goes steeply downhill behind the old Bond Store, alongside the peaty Ledaig (*Laychick*) burn and so to the main road.

Walk 2 Aros Park

Walk across the car park at the south side of the bay, past the distillery, garage and macGochans, to the beginning of a small path. A notice board tells you that this is the coastal path to Aros Park and Loch but that it is steep and slippery in places. If you are suitably shod, you will have a beautiful walk. **Aros Park** was created in the 1960s out of part of the large estate, including Tobermory itself, bought by the Allan family. This coastal path would originally have been used by estate workers as they went from Aros House (also called Drumfin) to the village, past **Sput Dubh** (*Sput Doo*), a waterfall cascading into the bay. This was used as the water supply for the ships of the Western Approaches Command. The Park is now run by the Forestry Commission and there is a good choice of walks, of varying lengths, well sign posted, within the Park.

A drive or walk round the top of the town

Driving or walking up the hill past the Distillery, the ruins of an 18th-century mill can be seen in the trees to the right. The door lintel of this is said to have come from the galleon sunk in the bay. Undoubtedly the wood is old but no more can be said for certain. There is also an old power house hidden away here. Turn left at the top and the Tobermory Fish Shop, interesting craft shops and coffee shop of **Baliscate** are on the right, a little way along. Further still, on the left of the main road, is The Children's Animal Farm. (See Box on Balamory). Go back to the little roundabout – the only one on the island – and carry straight on past new houses on your left. In about half a mile (804m) at the cross roads, turn right and, a short distance along, on your right, is a granite cross. This commemorates the coronation of Edward VII in 1902 and stands over the site of **St Mary's Well**. Water still flows from the fountain though the chained cup looks rather dubious! Opposite this is **Tobermory cemetery**, which is full of ancient grave stones, Celtic crosses, and the remains of the tiny medieval chapel just to the right of the kissing gate entrance.

Continue on a short way and turn right down Albert Street, left into Breadalbane Street and, when you come to the T junction, look to the left.

Mull Pottery

Situated on the Salen road into Tobermory. Hand thrown ceramics with designs inspired by the West Coast of Scotland. Gallery, café and restaurant serves local seafood and farm produce.

Baliscate, Tobermory PA75 6QA
☎ 01688 302347

Whisky

Modern distillery

At the south side of the bay is the **Tobermory Distillery**, which was built in 1798 by a local man who saw possibilities in the excellent water of the nearby burn. The distillery suffered mixed fortunes during the 19th century but, by the beginning of the 20th it was producing a malt whisky called 'Old Mull'. But the next 70 years saw numerous openings and closings of the distillery. During World War II the bond store was used as a barracks, ammunition store and canteen before being sold and turned into flats. Burn Stuart Distillers took over in 1993 and they now produce over 4,546,000 gallons (1,000,000L) a year. There is also a newer whisky, with a more peaty taste, called 'Iona' which is only available in Tobermory and on Iona. There is a Visitors' Centre and a shop.

History

Whisky was not popular in Mull until the early 18th century. Before this ale was a much more frequent drink. But, by 1736 an Act of Parliament had become necessary to prohibit the making of the 'water of life', partly because it was being distilled several times, turning it into such a strong brew that more than a little of it could kill! Naturally this Act was resented and illegal distilling started with smuggling becoming rife. Mull, with its many remote corners, soon had illicit stills, especially near the sea. In Gaelic 'water of life' was uisge beatha and the pronunciation sounding like 'ushgy' it soon evolved into the word 'whisky'.

Illicit stills

The illicit stills found in caves were all of a similar design. There would have had to be access for ponies to carry down the grain and the fuel needed for the fire. Quite often a wall of turf was built in front of the cave to disperse the smoke and hide the flames from the sea. Inside the cave, a platform was made with a hollow in it for the fire on which the distilling, or black, pot was placed. From the pot came the worm, a coiled metal tube that needed a nearby source of water to cool it. The whisky was put into kegs and carried up the cliff by the ponies or taken away by boat. Illicit distilling came to an end in the late 1820s when an Act was passed which held landowners guilty if a still was discovered on their property. Previously a blind eye had been turned to the practice as it provided cash whereby the tenants could pay their rents.

You will see the original manse, which was built to Thomas Telford's design in 1824. Turn left and follow the road round to the right, passing the school and the police station. At the end of this road you will see signs to the golf course. The road now becomes very narrow and it is not wise to continue by car as it is difficult to turn. Along here is the **Erray Farm House** where Boswell and Johnson stayed in 1773. Macleans owned it at this time and the ghost of the daughter, Mary, a most accomplished lady, is said to haunt the house!

Tobermory golf course is magnificently situated on top of the cliffs above the town. It is a nine-hole course with some very challenging holes. The present course was laid out in 1934, although it was originally founded in 1896. The Mull Highland Games have been held up here since 1923. There is a club house and visitors are always welcome. Clubs can be hired and all information can be obtained from Browns shop in the Main Street, near the Bank.

Walk 3 To the Lighthouse

A pleasant short walk is to the lighthouse called **Rubha-nan-Gall, Point of the Stranger**. At the north side of the bay, beyond the Cal-Mac pier by the lifeboat shed, is a path that meanders along the foot of the wooded cliffs. It can be slippery in wet weather but, with care, there should be no problem. Not long after the start you pass the site of Tobermory's bathing boxes, paddling pool and diving board! These have not been used for many years but some of the older inhabitants remember hearing of happy days spent in this area when children and adults must have been hardier! After about half an hour the lighthouse can be seen with views of the mouth of Loch Sunart and the north end of the Sound of Mull. The lighthouse was built in the 1850s and used until 1960. The keepers' cottages are now privately owned.

Glengorm

Leave Tobermory on the B8073, signposted Dervaig, and, at the cross roads, follow the small road straight on to **Glengorm Castle** about 4 miles (6.4km) distant. In half a mile (0.8km) there is a notice on your left to the **Glass Barn**. This is part of **Sgriobruadh** (*Skibrooa*) **Farm**. Sgriobruadh was awarded a Radio 4 Food and Farming Award in 2002 for their cheeses, which are made here and sent to outlets all over Britain. At certain times of the day you can watch the milking of sheep and cows and the processes of cheese making.

As you approach the Castle its silhouette against the sky can be forbidding or fairy-like depending upon the weather and your mood, but it is always dramatic. James Forsyth built the castle in the middle of the 19th century. He was one of the new Victorian landlords who had followed the fashion for buying Highland estates, often for their sporting opportunities. Extremely unpopular with his 260 tenants, who he felt were not sufficiently industrious, he made life impossible for many of them.

The story goes that, when his castle was built in 1858, he wished to call it 'Dunara' after an ancient ruin on the

Above: Mishnish Lochs

Below: The pencil tower at Dervaig Church is unique on Mull

Lighthouse, Rubha-nan-Gall

estate. An old woman bitterly remarked that he should call it 'Glengorm' which, delightedly, he did. He would not have been so pleased if he had realized that this meant 'Blue Glen' and was a reference to the days when the area had been blue with smoke from burning cottages. Forsyth died in 1862 never having lived in his new house. His wife spent the next 28 years living on Mull doing good works, perhaps to compensate for her husband's insensitivity and cruelty. The steadings have been converted into a farm shop and restaurant. There is also an exhibition gallery and ceramics shop.

Walk to Dun Ara

By the entrance to the Castle, a track forks to the left. Walk along here, turn right at some farm buildings and continue towards the coast. You will pass standing stones and, right on the coast, on **Sorne Point**, is a rocky outcrop on top of which was **Dun Ara castle**. Little is known about this but it is thought to have been a stronghold of the Mackinnons and to date from the 14th or 15th century. Not much remains, but to the expert eye there is evidence of the castle and outbuildings and, 100 yards (90m) or so to the south-west, a small bay with a jetty and boat noost or landing place. The view from here is spectacular, from Quinish Point on the left all round to Ardnamurchan Point, on the mainland, to the right. At the foot of the rocks is an ancient cairn.

Walk inland past An Sean Dun

Just before the standing stones, a track continues to the left. It passes nearby **An Sean Dun**, said to be one of the best preserved duns on Mull. After about 3 miles (4.8km) you will come out on the main B8073 road just beyond the Mishnish Lochs. From there it is about 4 miles (6.4km) to Tobermory in one direction and 4 miles (6.4km) to Dervaig in the other and you have probably left your car at Glengorm! However, the walk back to Glengorm along the track affords different views and is equally interesting.

Walk to ruined villages and the coast

Another walk starts at a Forestry Commission car park, close to the Tobermory end of the road from Tobermory to Glengorm. This goes out to **Ardmore Point** and passes the ruins of two villages on its way to the coast where a hide enables you to watch sea birds, seals and otters. There are also magnificent views out to other islands. On the coast to the right is **Bloody Bay**. It was here that, in 1480, a fierce battle was fought between John, 4th Lord of the Isles and Angus Og, his illegitimate son. Dozens of galleys filled the bay as the rivals closed in combat and before long the sea was red with blood as hundreds were killed. Around 50 of the defeated men took refuge in a cave but were smoked out and slaughtered by their enemies. Human skulls and other bones have been found in this area!

Tobermory to Dervaig

The drive along the B8073 from Tobermory to Dervaig is about 8 miles (12.9km). Less than a mile from Tobermory you will pass a house called **Newdale**. It was here that the **Mull Combination Poorhouse** was built in 1860. At one time it housed 140 people from Mull, Coll, Tiree and parts of the mainland. There was a joiner's shop, smithy, stables, byres, piggery and vegetable garden. The last inhabitants were taken to Oban in 1922 and it was pulled down in 1973.

The road runs past the **Mishnish** Lochs, where you may fish with a permit obtained from Brown's shop in Tobermory. Halfway along there is a ruined cottage right beside the road. The track behind this leads to a genuine volcanic crater with a tiny loch in it, and a circuit of this provides wonderful, peaceful views. The B8073 goes down a hill beyond the ruined cottage. At the bottom there is a new track to the left that takes you to the shores of **Loch Frisa**, the largest fresh water loch on Mull. It is possible to make a complete circuit of this loch — quite a long walk but well worth doing.

Dervaig

The B8073 continues through open moorland. Look out for eagles in this area but do not confuse them with buzzards, which are also large birds and can often be seen, frequently sitting on telephone posts watching for their next meal. Past the old shooting lodge of Achnadrish the road climbs steeply round several hairpin bends. From the top you can look to the left and glimpse Loch Frisa. Going down an equally steep and zigzag road into Dervaig you will have wide views in the other direction. There is a viewpoint just before the last descent and a track to standing stones hidden among the trees on the right. Part way down the hill is the old cemetery with a few traces of the ancient **Chapel of Kilmore** in it and one old tombstone which might give the reader an initial shock for, after the name of the lady, it reads 'Spouse To All'. Read on and you see that the sculptor ran out of space and had to put the 'an' on the next line!

The village of Dervaig was planned in 1799 by Alexander Maclean of Coll. He had 13 pairs of cottages built, each with its own garden and grazing on the hill. When James Forsyth bought the estate in 1857 he raised rents and removed the grazing ground making life impossible for the crofters. Today the village has a pub, two shops – in one of which you can get coffee and a wide selection of books – a hotel, a large new village hall and an interesting church. The latter is on the left as you go out of the village. Its tapering pencil tower is unique on Mull. Inside, the church is quiet, relaxing and has a feeling of warmth. The painted ceiling of the apse is strikingly beautiful and, although 100 years old, it has not faded. The design of the interior was influenced by the 'Arts and Crafts Movement' and the symbols on this ceiling are characteristic of the period. The stained glass windows are also of a high quality. By the church a road to the left cuts across the island and in about 10 miles (16.1km) reaches the Salen to Tobermory road at Aros Bridge. (See later.) A quarter of a mile along this road is the original site of **Mull Little Theatre**.

On to Calgary

From here you can continue along this small road, back to Aros Bridge and thence to Tobermory, or you can return to the B8073 and continue over the river Bellart and around the head of **Loch Cuin** (*Cooan*). In half a mile (0.8km) there is a left hand turn to Torloisk. Once again, make a diversion here and follow the signs to The **Old Byre Heritage Centre** where you can sample home cooking and visit the exhibition gallery. A 30-minute film will give you an enjoyable insight into Mull's history. There are also showcases illustrating this, and some of the wild life to be found on the island.

Returning to the Calgary road, in a couple of miles (3.2km) there is a right turning to **Croig**. This road finishes at an old stone pier and small bay, which was an ancient landing place for cattle brought from Coll and Tiree. They were herded over the drove roads of Mull to Grasspoint, which is the nearest part of the island to the mainland. Two hundred years ago Croig had a post office and a drovers' inn. If you can leave your car somewhere out of the way, there are walks and lovely sandy bays down here.

As you continue on the B8073 towards Calgary look to your right. On a good day it is possible to see many islands, including Rum, Eigg, Muck and Canna. Another right turn goes only to **Sunipol**. The 22-year-old Thomas Campbell spent the summer of 1795 tutoring five children at Sunipol Farm and wrote *The Pleasures of Hope* whilst there. He found Mull boring but as he was a young man in an out-of-the-way spot, perhaps this is not surprising! Again, there are many walks, magnificent coastal views, ruined villages, duns, standing stones and wildlife of all kinds in this area.

Just before Calgary Bay is the **Carthouse Gallery.** Local artists and crafts people exhibit here and there are refreshments, as well as an 'Art in Nature'

Above: *Calgary Bay*   **Below:** *Boathouse visitor's centre, Ulva, from Ulva Ferry*

trail through the woods. You will need stout footwear as the paths are steep in places and can be muddy but there is an abundance of wild flowers, birds and other wildlife to be seen, as well as sculptures hidden up in the trees, in the pond or tucked into clearings. Adults and children alike will find this an unusual walk.

Coming down the hill, **Calgary Bay** opens before you with its immense expanse of white sand. On the left **Calgary House**, or **Calgary Castle**, can be seen among the trees. It was built in the 1820s and is a smallish castellated Gothic mansion. Captain Allan McAskill, the builder of the house, left it to his nephew who cleared crofters off the land until, by 1840, several dozen families had been moved. As you drive

up the south side of the bay stop and look across to the north where you might be able to spot one of the ruined villages, some 250 ft (76m) above the sea. Be careful where you pause here as the road is very narrow and passing places are just that – not parking places. In fact, it is better to leave your car by the public toilets and walk on up the hill to admire the wonderful view of the bay, hopefully sparkling in the sun.

Calgary in Canada takes its name from here, not the other way round. A Commissioner of the Canadian Mounties had been a guest in Calgary Castle. He enjoyed his visit so much that when he returned to Canada he named one of the outposts established by the Mounties, 'Fort Calgary'. This grew into Calgary, Alberta.

Moorlands and ruined villages

The next stretch of road is fascinating but the driver will not be able to appreciate it as much as his passengers! The road hugs the rocks, twisting and turning as it switchbacks, until you round the final corner and turn inland where miles of desolate moorland open before you. Standing starkly in the middle of this is an isolated building. Once this was a school with the teacher's rooms on the first floor. It has recently been made into a private house.

Some of the best walks in the north of Mull can be found round here. Walkers are welcome but do not take cars along privately owned tracks

Below: *Kilninian Church*

and remember that the whole area is farming land – dogs must be kept on a lead at all times. It is possible to become so mesmerized by the views, birds, flora and fauna that you walk on and on.

Isolated school

Reudle school was built around 1860 to serve the several villages which then existed in the area. Children often had miles to walk and sometimes carried with them a peat block to put on the fire. There are drawings of ships in full sail, initials and dates, on the wall of the school room, perhaps done by bored pupils, or even their teacher! The school closed around 1877 as the villages gradually became depopulated.

Even a bad day holds its own dramatic charm as showers scud in across the wide seascape and waves pound the distant islands and echo in the caves below you.

Walk to ruined villages and the whisky cave

This walk can be done in either direction and may be made as long as you wish. It takes in the ruined village of **Crackaig**, the whisky cave and **Haun**. Leave your car off the road, a little way down the hill from the access to the old school. The track across the moor is boggy in parts so be suitably shod. Follow the contour of the hill making towards the sea. After about a mile (1.6km) you will find two deserted villages, the lower one, Crackaig, being

particularly interesting. Up to the early 19th century 200 people lived here, by 1861 there were 53 and by 1886 only six were left – disease, wars and famine had taken their toll. Look for initials and dates scratched on some of the houses. The village, which had a communal garden near the burn and old ash tree, was built on a plateau above steep cliffs.

If you go down you will be well rewarded as you arrive on a four-mile-long (6.4km) raised beach from which you can see the **Treshnish Islands** and look even further down to the sea below you. With patience you might even spot otters swimming through the clear water, a wonderful and unusual sight. Shags occupy the many caves and other sea birds are plentiful. Turn to the right and follow the path through the bracken until, in about a mile (1.6km), you see a narrow, steep gully with a stony beach. Tucked back into the cliff is the whisky cave with the remnants of the still inside. It is possible to continue along the raised beach to Haun and the House of Treshnish and so back to the road.

Loch Tuath

Beyond Reudle school the road returns to the sea and turns east. As you travel along this coast, across **Loch Tuath** are the islands of **Ulva** and **Gometra**. Look out for the point at which you can clearly see the causeway that links them. Between the road and the sea are many archaeological remains such as cairns, forts and duns. The best of the latter is **Dun Aisgain** (*Ayshgain*), which is a galleried dun, sadly crumbling away, but it is over 2,000 years old after all!

Kilninian church stands a little back from the road. It was built in 1755 on the site of a mediaeval chapel and is the oldest church building and was still in use until quite recently. There are many fine carved stones in the vestry, one bearing the full length effigy of a man in armour with his claymore, another with a pair of shears carved on it and a third with a comb and mirror. The mid-18th-century table tombs and Maclean shields are worth examining. See if you can find the late mediaeval mass dial.

The path just to the west of the church goes over the hill to the old school at Mornish, about 1 miles (2.4km) east of Calgary bay. It is an old track which must have been well used, particularly by churchgoers from the villages around Calgary. On a good day, as you walk over, the views both behind and in front, are extensive but remember you have to walk back, or have someone meet you at the other end.

A mile beyond Kilninian church the hill road from Dervaig joins the B8073. At this junction is **Torloisk House**, which has been privately owned since the middle of the 19th century by the same family – the Comptons. Historically it is of great interest and has been visited by many famous people.

Beyond Torloisk the road commands splendid views as it winds its way southeast along Loch Tuath. Near the farm of Kilbrenan is another fine broch, or

Torloisk

In the early 1780s Lachlan Maclean of Torloisk built a new house beside the simple one that was on the site. The eminent French geologist, Faujas de St Fond, called it a 'commodious habitation' when he visited in 1784. He was impressed by Lachlan's daughter, Marianne, who was pretty, graceful, talented, modest and played the harpsichord well. Marianne inherited the house and had it considerably altered and improved. She was friendly with Sir Walter Scott who visited Torloisk and introduced the son of the Marquis of Northampton to one of her daughters. They married and the house still belongs to the same family.

The Pirate of Torloisk.

Legend says that in the 16th century an illegitimate son was born to a daughter of the family at Torloisk. To punish her she was made to work as a servant. A witch put a spell on the girl so that the pregnancy lasted 15 months but eventually the baby was born on a rough straw bed. His first act was to grasp a handful of straw and suck it. Thereafter he was known as Allan of the Straws. Allan was so persecuted by his mother's family that he ran away to join one of the Danish pirate ships terrorizing the neighbourhood at that time. He soon became a feared pirate, ravaging and pillaging the western seas. After many years he left his life of marauding, married and settled down at Torloisk. He is buried on Iona.

Loch na Keal

first century fortification, where you can still see traces of the stairway in the thickness of the wall and bar holes at the entrance. The broch stands in a field that is reputed to be cursed!

The **Eas Fors waterfall** appears in the film *Where Eight Bells Toll*. There is a rock pool at the foot of the lower fall, which can only be approached along the shore. Behind is a cave that is dif-ficult to enter because of the thundering water. Tradition says that this was where a local piper used to come to compose his tunes, far from the ears of rivals. Apparently, pipers guarded their compositions so jealously that anyone who stole a tune ran the risk of assault, or even murder!

Just after Ulva Ferry Primary school and the turning down to **Ulva Ferry**

Lord Ullin

Lord Ullin was said to be Sir Allan Maclean of Knock on Mull. His daughter was eloping to Ulva with the son of the Chief of this island when a storm blew up and they were drowned. They were probably using the long crossing from Gribun to Ulva, which was the usual route for those days. It crosses Loch na Keal which can become extremely stormy and dangerous under certain conditions. Thomas Campbell used poetic license and altered the names in his famous poem:

Now who be ye, would cross Lochgyle

This dark and stormy water?

O I'm the chief of Ulva's isle,

And this, Lord Ullin's daughter.

Eas Fors Waterfall

Aros Castle and the Sound of Mull

itself, there is a track to a fish farm. A modern monument commemorating Lord Ullin's Daughter has been erected down here. It stands in the middle of a bog and is already rather dilapidated.

Loch na Keal to Aros

Back up the hill, the B8073 follows the north side of **Loch na Keal**. Across the loch you can see the stark, distinctive outline of the **Gribun** (*Greebun*) rocks with a tiny thread of road clinging to the base. On a clear day, Ben More, Mull's highest mountain, may condescend to show you its full height, shouldering its way above its lesser brethren. In the middle of the loch is the small, uninhabited island of Eorsa, whilst on the right lies **Inch Kenneth**. Behind this, the Ross of Mull traces a line on the horizon with Iona's white sands catching the sun at the end. Loch na Keal was an important anchorage for naval ships in both World Wars.

At the head of Loch na Keal is a camp site in what is surely one of the loveliest of positions. The estate of **Killiechronan** runs this, and pony trekking. The house itself is a little further on just at a point where you will be carefully negotiating a tricky bend round the boundary wall! Turn left at the T-junction to Salen (*Sahlen*). This village will be dealt with later, so turn left in the village and after a mile you will be at **Aros Bridge**. As you approach you will see the ruins of **Aros Castle** and, below it, the **White House** of **Aros** on the promontory.

Aros Bridge used to be one of the most important areas on Mull. Nearby was an inn, a mill, and several cottages.

An early post office opened in 1786 and the travelling court house was held here. The old Aros bridge, which is no longer used, was one of the first on the island.

It is hard to credit that, had it not been for the battle of Culloden in 1745, this area might have become the site of an Academy of Mull. Just before the battle, a group of prominent men had gathered to discuss a scheme for the establishment of an academy or grammar school here for Highland students who, otherwise, had to travel many miles on the mainland. As travel was then slow, difficult, dangerous and expensive, this idea would undoubtedly have been of great value and encouragement to learning and would have been followed through. However, it was not to be. The plan was lost in the ensuing battle, which swept away, for ever, the Highland ways and economy.

As you travel north back to Tobermory look down to the right. All along here there used to be groups of cottages or townships with millers, blacksmiths, tailors and weavers amongst them. There are several cairns, a broch and standing stones. For the archaeologist and historian it is a part of the island that has many stories to tell but most of us travel as quickly as we can through it nowadays. At the highest point of the new double track road there is a view point called **Gualan Dhubh** (*Gulan Doo*). The panorama from here takes in Tobermory, Ardnamurchan with Ben Hiant, Kilhoan and part of Morvern. There is a small loch behind you. Sit on the seat and absorb the peace and tranquillity before returning to Tobermory.

Aros Castle

Aros Castle has had a varied and turbulent history. It was probably built in the 1200s by MacDougall, Lord of Lorne. In 1314 MacDonald, Lord of the Isles, captured it. Their tenure lasted 180 years until Macleans ousted them. Around 1674 it was the turn of the Campbell clan to own the castle! Since then it has been quietly crumbling away, some of its stones being reused in nearby cottages. The ruins are now privately owned and are dangerous. It is better to view them from a distance and give your imagination free rein in reconstructing its past.

Aros Castle was actually a Hall House, 28 x 14yd (25.6 x 12.8m) wide with walls 4–12ft (1.2–3.7m) thick. There was a curtain wall, which enclosed the bailey and one or two other buildings within it and, at one end of the castle is a square latrine tower. In 1540 King James V made a voyage around his kingdom and summoned the rebellious island Chiefs to confer with him on board his ship, which was anchored below the castle. He then took them captive. They were only released much later on assurances of good conduct and co-operation. Much later, in 1608, another meeting of island chiefs was held at the castle. This time it was James VI who sent an emissary to make clear his intentions that the islands should be made to conform with the laws of the rest of his kingdom. His attempts made little difference in the long run.

In the 17th, 18th and 19th centuries many visitors were rowed or sailed to Mull. Very often they landed at the pier near the White House of Aros where there was a small inn with a number of cottages in the area. On the hill above stood Aros Mains house and it was from here that the approaching boats could be seen and preparations rapidly made to welcome the visitors. Some called it a grim gothic building, others called it a very good house; perhaps the weather affected their assessments! The house has been altered and added to but is substantially as it always was. It is said to be haunted by a ghost, which has been seen in recent years.

Salen (Sahlen) is a small village at the narrowest part of Mull. At this point the island is only three miles (4.8km) across. Salen has one shop, a post office, hotel, many bed and breakfasts, garage, petrol pumps, police station, doctor's surgery and a thriving primary school. The only hospital on the island is just out of the village on the Gruline road.

Medieval carved cross-shaft in the ruins of Pennygowan Chapel

a community, which he planned to call 'Port Macquarie'. But he never changed the name.

The **Church of Scotland** dominates the middle of the village today. In all, there have been four churches on this site starting 300 years ago when a

Until the beginning of the 19th century Salen was a collection of cottages with a tiny inn and a small church. Then, Major General Lachlan Macquarie (*see later*) bought many acres of land including Salen. He established tradesmen here, giving them land on which to build their own cottages, improving the inn and making the area into

Thomas Telford

Thomas Telford was a civil engineer, born in Scotland in 1757. By the time he was 30 he had been appointed Surveyor of Public Works in Shropshire where he was responsible for designing and building many bridges, aqueducts, and public buildings. In 1790 he moved to Scotland where roads, piers, bridges and canals were built to his plans. In the 1820s he was asked by the Government to design new churches and manses all over Scotland. On Mull there are two Telford, or Parliamentary, churches, plus one on Ulva and one on Iona.

Salen church bell and the mystery of the grave

The Salen church bell hangs on a wooden structure in the churchyard. It was given in 1834 by Richard Alsager of Surrey. He was an interesting man who had spent all his life at sea with the East India Company. Eventually he became a Captain and made many journeys to India and China, retiring finally in 1827. He and his wife lived in Tooting and Richard was elected to Parliament in 1835. He remained an MP until his death in 1841. Why he came to Salen in 1834 is a matter for speculation. One other mystery concerns Salen church. Behind the building is a patch of rough ground that is said to mark the site of a grave, an unusual position for such a thing. No-one is absolutely sure who lies here although some suggestions have been made. Considerable research has been inconclusive and the mystery of the grave remains.

small one was built. By 1777 a slightly larger building was felt to be necessary; in 1824, a bigger one still was needed and the present church was erected in 1899. Opposite, down a private drive, can be glimpsed the manse which was designed by Thomas Telford and built in 1828.

The building now called '**Argyll House**' was the original inn and 'The Craig', opposite, was a shop with a big window in the front. 'Craig' means 'rock' and tradition says that St Columba stood on the huge rock beside the house to preach his gospel.

By Salen hotel a turning to the left takes you past the surgery and primary school and ends at the pier. This is now privately owned and is derelict and sad but in its heyday it was a scene of bustling activity. Before the deep water pier at Craignure, the ferries from Oban used to call to load and unload passengers, freight, cows, sheep, horses and a few cars. It was near here that the 'fever hospital' stood, well away from the road, in a bog held down by wires

and rocks! Its only inhabitants ever were a roadman, his wife, a hen and chickens, and in 1927 it was blown into the sea – without its inhabitants – and was never seen again.

You may notice some pieces of wood sticking out of the sea about halfway down the pier road. These are all that remain of an even older pier, last used at the beginning of the 20th century. On the Craignure road out of the village you will see a sign to '**Salen Silver**' where you will find locally crafted items for sale.

Beyond the **Glenforsa air strip** is **Pennygown burial ground** with a roofless mediaeval chapel in it. There are interesting grave stones here, some extremely old, and various legends concerning the chapel roof. One of these says that in the 17th century black magic was practised and this is why the roof did not stay on. Another story insists that each night fairies, who lived in the green mound nearby, removed whatever had been built during the day, but as these were good fairies who also obligingly completed whatever work was left out for them, it seems unlikely that they dismantled the roof! However that maybe, Pennygown is a peaceful place now, with a beautiful view up the Sound of Mull.

About halfway between Salen and Craignure is **Balmeanach Park** with a caravan and camping site and also a licensed tearoom. Just beyond is a left turning to the **Fishnish ferry** which goes across to Lochaline on Morvern. In the 18th and 19th centuries there were several villages and a well-attended school in the area which is now covered by Forestry Commission trees. An old jetty can still be seen, to the east of the present one, where cattle were ferried over at a charge, in 1828, of 2/- (10p) for a bull and 6d (2p) for a cow! Forest Enterprise has recently marked out walks of varying lengths, which start from the car park at Fishnish.

Further along, the A849 runs close to the sea around **Scallastle bay** which has been the scene of stirring and terrible events. In 1690, ships carrying troops anchored here. They had been sent to 'persuade' the Chiefs to swear allegiance to William and Mary. As punishment for their refusal to do so, the ordinary people living nearby suffered – cottages were burnt, crops destroyed and cattle killed. It was here, too, where Government ships anchored when searching for Bonnie Prince Charlie.

Scallastle was once an important area. The original house was burned down in the 18th century but it was rebuilt and had the most beautiful garden and orchard in Mull. There was once a brewery here and the house itself frequently gave hospitality to passing visitors. The land in this area was good arable land but, by 1836, the house stood empty.

Just before Craignure is Craignure golf course – quite a challenging links course with magnificent views over the Sound of Mull.

Craignure

Craignure has been the main terminal for the ferry from Oban since the mid 1960s. Before this, the ferry anchored in deep water whilst goods and passengers were off-loaded into small boats

Wartime wreck

As you go along the road towards Craignure look out for a prominent mountain on your right. This is **Ben Talaidh** (*Tala*), around 2400ft (732m) high. In February 1945, a Dakota of RAF Transport Command, flying from Canada to Prestwick, crashed on this mountain. The weather was atrocious, the worst that had been known for many years. A dozen people from Salen, including the local doctor, climbed through appalling conditions to the rescue. Five of the eight people on board were saved and Dr Flora MacDonald and several others were recognised for their courage. There are still pieces of the wreckage scattered on the mountain side and a bothy which holds a visitors' book where people who wish to remember the dead, have signed their names.

Above and inset: Torosay Castle

The Great Mull Air Mystery

At **Glenforsa**, half a mile (0.8km) from Salen, is the tiny air strip used by private planes and in medical emergencies. Each year there is an air weekend when a number of light aircraft gather and all is activity. The strip itself has to be cleared of sheep in the winter whenever it is to be used. It was made in 1965 by the Royal Engineers and, 10 years later it became the focus of the Great Mull Air Mystery.

At Christmas 1975 Peter Gibbs, a 54-year-old ex Spitfire pilot, hired a Cessna 150 and flew to Mull. His licence had lapsed and his eyesight was not too good but, late on Christmas Eve, he took off into the darkness from the tiny strip, which he knew had no landing lights to guide him back. It began to snow and the plane never returned. For days a huge air, sea and mountain search took place but not the tiniest clue as to his fate could be found. Four months later a body was discovered 400ft (12.2m) up a hill and this was identified as Peter Gibbs. There were no injuries on the body. Years later the plane was found in the Sound of Mull but the mystery of why he took off and how his body came to be so far up the hillside has never been solved.

Narrow gauge railway, Craignure

and landed on the old jetty, which is still there. Queen Elizabeth II, the Duke of Edinburgh and Princess Margaret came this way in 1956.

There is a tourist office, post office, shop, restaurant, inn, police station, garage and petrol pumps in Craignure.

There are also bed and breakfasts, as well as a camp site with self-catering 'shielings', boat, canoe and bicycle hire and the possibility of activities such as archery and abseiling.

Just as you go into Craignure, on the left by the Isle of Mull Hotel, there is a new swimming pool.

If you go past the village hall and the camp site you will find something unique. This is Scotland's only **island railway** – a 10 inch gauge line which goes to Torosay Castle, a 20-minute ride away. The journey follows the coast giving a superb sea and mountain panorama with Ben Nevis, the Glencoe Hills and Ben Cruachan in the background. You can ride both ways, being pulled by either diesel or steam, or you can walk one way through the woods.

Duart Castle

Torosay

Torosay Castle is further along the A849 which now becomes single track.

Torosay Castle is a Scottish baronial style mansion built in the 1850s. The house is full of family scrap books, portraits and memorabilia which can be examined at leisure in a relaxed atmosphere. You can even sit down to enjoy things to the full. From the windows are magnificent views across the gardens and the bay to Duart Castle. The 12 acres (4.9ha) of Torosay gardens contain a walk lined with 18th-century Italianate statues, formal terraces, a woodland garden and pool, an alpine garden, rock and bog areas, a Japanese garden and much more. Torosay is also a working farm with pedigree highland cattle. To complete your day there is a tearoom with delicious home baking. (Open daily 10.30am–5.00pm Easter to end-October. Gardens open all year.)

Duart

The turning to **Duart Castle** is clearly signposted further on. It is a narrow road and, at certain times of the day, can be busy. Please be patient and prepared to back. Duart Castle stands in a dramatic position on its great cliff, frowning out over the bay, proudly guarding the Sound of Mull as it has done for hundreds of years. Many battles have been fought within, around and over the Castle since the 13th and 14th centuries. In the late 17th century it became derelict and remained so until Sir Fitzroy Maclean bought it back and restored it at the beginning of the 20th century. It has been the home of the Clan Maclean ever since. The present Chief, Sir Lachlan, is the 28th. His father, Lord Maclean, was Lord Chamberlain of the Queen's Household and also Chief Scout of the Commonwealth.

A visit to this splendid castle is a must. From the kitchens and dank dungeon, through the magnificent Great Hall and up to the battlements you can re-live the past with its terrors and tragedies, its triumphs and victories. For centuries the fortunes of the Campbells and Macleans ebbed and flowed and the castle changed hands several times. During the 1650s ships were sent by Cromwell to capture the Chief of the Macleans who was only 10 years old. A great storm sank three of these, directly below the castle, within sight and hearing of those on land. One of the wrecks, The Swan, is being monitored by the Institute of Maritime Studies at St Andrews University. You can read about the on-going work in the castle. The history of the Clan Maclean is also displayed and there are objects of historical interest wherever you go. When you have thoroughly explored the Castle you can drink in the majestic view or go into the well-stocked shop and tearoom to refresh yourself with home baking. (Open daily 10.30am–6.30pm, May to mid October.)

Looking from the Castle windows, south of Lismore, is a tidal reef with a warning beacon on it. It was here, in the middle of the 15th century, that a Duart Chief had his wife, daughter of the 2nd Earl of Argyll and whom he no longer loved, marooned and left to drown. Unknown to the Chief she was rescued by a passing fishing boat and was returned to her own family on the mainland. Years later, her brother took his revenge by stabbing the Chief to death.

Lochdonhead

Continue along the A849 to the small settlement of Lochdonhead where there is a primary school, a tiny post office (rather hidden!) and a road to Grasspoint. You may wish to follow this road although it goes nowhere else. If you do, in a few yards look to your left and you will see a small church. This is the **Free Church of Scotland**. In the tiny graveyard is a memorial to a Postal Telegraph Service worker who lost his life on the hills nearby in 1879.

In 1843, at the Disruption, many members of the Established Church of Scotland left to form the Free Church. Some of these new congregations were persecuted and unable to find land on which to build their own church. In many places worship had to be held in the open air, and on the mainland, one congregation had an iron floating church built. The ship-church sank one inch (2.54cm) for every 100 who attended and sometimes there was a depression of six inches (15.24cm) or more! At Lochdonhead the Free Church congregation had to meet in a gravel pit, which was sometimes flooded at high tide! They met in rain, hail, wind or snow, occasionally with water lapping round their ankles. After many years they were granted land and the Free church was opened in 1852. The gravel pit, overgrown now, is across the road from the building with a rope swing hanging from a tree and a small stream trickling across the middle. Present day children play there, where once their ancestors worshipped in defiance of all hardship.

The road to Grasspoint is small, winding and beautiful. Together with the bridge at its start it is one of the oldest roads on Mull, as Grasspoint was once an important ferry place, being the nearest part of Mull to the mainland. For centuries cattle were transferred to the mainland from here, via the island of Kerrara. Dozens of drovers would converge bringing hundreds of cattle from Mull, Coll, Tiree and even further away. At Grasspoint their beasts were either loaded into small boats or swum over to Kerrara, walked across to a second ferry and then ferried or swum to the mainland near Oban. For many years there was an inn and a post office, with its own postmark, at **Grasspoint**. Until comparatively recently the Sunday papers were landed here from a small boat, as there was no other ferry that day. Occasionally passengers might be allowed to join the papers if they were stranded in Oban!

Returning to the A 849, about 3 miles (5.6km) further on is a road to Lochbuie and Croggan. Set on the hill at this junction is a **memorial to Dugald MacPhail** (see later).

Loch Spelve

Turn on to the Lochbuie road and, up the hill look out for a seat on the left with a wishing well opposite. The road runs by **Loch Spelve**, a sea loch, and then passes **Loch Uisg** (Ushk), a fresh water loch surrounded by woods and rhododendrons, which are perfectly reflected in the tranquil surface. At the end of this second loch is a lodge where

Above and right: Mull's only stone circle and huge standing stone

the road sweeps to the right and then in a wide arc, back to the left towards the sea.

Rare stone circle

Just before the left hand sweep is a notice by a gate on the left, which tells you to follow the white stones that mark the footpath to a stone circle. Mull has many standing stones – most stand alone, some are grouped in twos or threes, but this is the only circle. It is nearly 40ft (12m) across and originally consisted of nine stones but only eight remain, the tallest being over 6ft (1.8m) in height. At certain times of the year the growth of vegetation and bracken spoils the impressiveness of this enigmatic place. It is best in winter when the low rays of the sun add to its mystery and atmosphere.

Lochbuie

The road finishes at Lochbuie but there is much to be seen by exploring on foot. Having parked the car, walk along the track to the east, past the small **church of St Kilda**, which is privately owned, and on to the shore. You will have a good view of **Lochbuie House** and, further on, of **Moy Castle**. These are both privately owned. Even further to the east is the wide sweep of Laggan sands, backed by grass and gorse. On the far side is a tiny chapel or mausoleum in which are memorial tablets to the Maclaine family of Lochbuie. The building is basically mediaeval in date but was completely restored in 1864 and again in 1972. In its ceiling are set green, red, white, orange and blue pieces of glass in the shape of stars through which the natural light is diffused into richly hued patterns on the walls and floor.

Beyond the mausoleum the ground is rough. This eastern side of Lochbuie is rarely explored but here you may spot wild goats whilst, along the impressive southern coastline, is **Lord Lovat's cave** – 300ft (91m) long, 40ft (12.2m) wide and varying in height from 40 to 100ft (12.2 to 30.5m). Lord Lovat hid here for two years after the battle of Culloden.

Moy Castle

Moy Castle is mostly early 15th century. It was built by Hector, brother of Lachlan Maclean of Duart, who wanted his own property. It was not until over 300 years later that the Lochbuie branch began spelling their name 'Maclaine'. Alterations and additions were made to the Castle in succeeding centuries. It is now kept locked as the ruins are dangerous but it can be examined from outside. Note the battlemented parapet, the latrine chutes and the chimney stack. Inside are the

Moy castle with Ben More in the background

Lochbuie legend

The legend of the Black Horse concerns the Lochbuie House of today. Whenever death or disaster is about to strike a member of the family, the sound of galloping hooves is heard. As recently as the mid-20th century a local doctor was attending one of the family. As he drove to the house he heard a horse gallop towards him and pulled his car to one side to let it pass. The sound of hooves came, passed and receded but he saw nothing. Two days later his patient died.

remains of a well, and a pit prison descending deep underground. Outside was a courtyard and a boat-landing to the south.

After abandoning Moy Castle, the Maclaines lived in a small house built in 1752. This still stands as part of the outbuildings behind the present house and was where Boswell and Johnson stayed in 1773. They described it as poor, but at least it had two floors! The present **Lochbuie House** was built in the late 18th century and consisted of a central portion of three floors with two wings at the sides. The bow-fronted part was a later addition. Inside the house is the wrought-iron grill which once protected the doorway of Moy Castle.

Walk 1: Lochbuie to Carsaig

If you are a good walker, suitably shod and equipped, it is possible to walk from Lochbuie to Carsaig along the coast to the west. By road it is well over 20 miles (32.2km) but only six (9.7km) by the shore. But, unless you have someone to meet you, remember that you will have to walk back as well! For the first two miles (3.2km), until you reach the ruined farm of Glenbyre, there is a track. After this the going becomes harder as the cliffs come closer to the sea and your path becomes boulder strewn. It is especially awkward at high tide. After about two miles (3.2km) of this difficult section the going becomes easier but muddy until you reach Carsaig Pier. Even if you only do the first part of the walk you will find it rewarding with the sea, the birds and dramatic and varied scenery to accompany you. But do take care as even the best walker can slip – and remember to watch the tide.

Walk 2: Lochbuie to Glenmore

Another, completely different and less adventurous walk, takes you inland from Lochbuie. It starts by the bridge near the sign to the stone circle. On the other side of the road is a track leading into the hills. In a couple of miles (3.2km) you pass three small lochs and then a short scramble brings you up to the main road through Glen More. Again, unless you are met you will need to walk back but the views are different and equally majestic so it should be no hardship. Small waterfalls, peaceful hollows and ever changing cloud shadows on the hillsides make this walk a popular one.

The Lochbuie area has something for everyone, of most ages and interests, including trying to find the post office!

The Mull Anthem

Dugald MacPhail was born in 1818 not far from where this memorial stands. At first he was a joiner but he studied drawing and mathematics and left Mull to become a clerk and draughtsman with an architect in Newcastle-on-Tyne. It was here, amongst the streets and houses, that his home sickness compelled him to write a poem to his homeland of Mull. For 15 years he and his wife and growing family lived in Newcastle and then they moved to Dorset, where he worked for the Marquis of Shaftesbury. Later they returned to Edinburgh with their five sons and three daughters, all of whom did well in medicine or religion. During his life Dugald MacPhail composed many songs and poems, but the one for which he is most famous is An t-eilean Muileach – The Island of Mull, composed in Newcastle. This has come to be regarded as the 'Mull Anthem' and is known and sung wherever there are Muileachs, as people from Mull are called. The first verse goes, in translation:

The Isle of Mull is of isles the fairest,

Of ocean's gems 'tis the first and rarest;

Green grassy island of sparkling fountains,

Of waving woods and high tow'ring mountains.'

Croggan

At the narrow neck of land that separates the salt water of Loch Spelve from the fresh water of Loch Uisg, are a Telford manse and a Telford church both of which are now private houses. The road to **Croggan** is a small one running right beside the shore. In about three miles (4.8km) you will find **Croggan pier** and a few houses set back under the hill. It is hard to believe that this pier was once active with steamers calling to land and load goods, people and animals. There was also a post office and a school.

Beyond here the road becomes a track, still close to the sea, which eventually turns the corner of the coast and ends at a house called **Portfield**. This is in a beautiful spot with wide views of the Firth of Lorne and the chance to see otters, seals, eagles and much else if you are quiet and patient. One would have needed a sturdy pair of legs, a good boat and the ability to be self-sufficient to live your life here. However, if you walk up the hillside away from the sea and cut inland back to Croggan, you will find the ruins of several villages which reminds us that once this area was not as isolated and lonely as it is now.

3. Central Mull - Glen More to Gruline

The road through Glen More passes through some of the wildest and grandest scenery on Mull. Depending upon your mood and the weather it can look gloomy, forbidding and frightening or wild and romantic or grand, glorious and liberating – perhaps all of these within a few moments. Nowadays there are only two houses in the whole glen that have roofs on them and the road, built in the 1960s, takes thousands of tourists to Iona. But once there were many inhabited settlements and dozens of tracks and drove roads criss-crossing the hills, along which cattle came in hundreds on their long journey to the markets of the mainland.

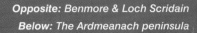
The old road with its attractive bridges can easily be picked out, sometimes on one side of the present one and sometimes on the other. Less easy to spot are the much older drove roads winding their way, sometimes 200ft (61m) up, around the contours of the hills. It was probably along one of these that John Keats came in 1818 when he stayed two nights in the glen in very poor accommodation. He called it a most dreary track!

Near the Lochbuie turning and the monument to Dugald MacPhail, you will find a little of the pre-1960 road. It is pleasant to wander peacefully down here and, after a short way, there is a small cairn near the river, with an iron cross on it. This is known as the **Pedlar's Grave**. The story behind it has sometimes been romanticized but, even without this, it is sad.

The small island in the loch by the inhabited house is a crannog, that is a man-made fortified island connected, in this case, to the shore by a causeway, which can be seen if the water is low. It was probably built in the 15th or 16th century and was used by the Maclaine family of Lochbuie. From the watershed at the top of the hill you will see a string of three lochs. It is by the side of these that it is possible to walk through to Lochbuie. Whatever time of day or year, whatever the weather, the view from here is majestic.

As you sweep down the road towards **Loch Scridain** there is a good view of the 'back' of Ben More on the right. At the bottom of the hill, by the lovely **Coladoir River** and its two-arched bridge, is a right turn along the B8035. This road follows the north side of Loch Scridain for two or three miles (3.2–4.8km) and then turns inland through Glen Seilisdeir (*Chilister*). Before continuing up here, take the left fork by a converted church. In about 1.5 miles (2.4km) the road goes through a yard with gates. Make sure these are closed after you and continue, carefully, on a very rough road. Eventually there will be a car park on the right. From here it is Shanks's pony!

Ardmeanach

This area of Mull is called Ardmeanach or Burg and its north-western side is so rough and rocky that it is often referred to as 'the wilderness'. The whole peninsula is composed of lava flows, which have been eroded into shallow steps. Embedded in the lowest of these layers, down at shore level, is a fossilized tree. It is about five miles (8km) to this and the last two (3km) are rough and difficult. You need to be properly shod and clothed, have food, drinks and extra clothing and let someone know where

Ladies from Ardmeanach

Daisy Cheape

On 15 August 1896, 12-year-old Daisy Cheape set out from Tiroran across the loch to Pennyghael in an open boat. There were nine people in the boat – two of Daisy's older brothers, her younger sister and five adults including two boatmen. The Cheape family owned both the estates of Carsaig and Tiroran. The wind was strong and a sudden squall turned the boat over, drowning Daisy and one of the adults, both good swimmers. All the rest, including three dogs, were saved. Daisy's grave is at Carsaig but this hill, one of her favourite places, she called her 'Castle Dare' in reference to a novel by William Black. The monument was erected in 1910.

Chrissie MacGillivray

For many people, residents and visitors alike, this part of Mull will always be associated with a lady called Chrissie MacGillivray or 'Chrissie Burg'. She was born in 1898, the sixth child of eight, and lived in Burg farm for most of her life, and died there in 1989. As a child Chrissie walked barefoot along the rough and steep track to Scobull school, still to be seen near Tiroran House Hotel. Chrissie worked for a while away from home but returned to look after her parents and then her youngest brother. She was a cheerful, happy, hard working lady with such a warm and hospitable personality that she is remembered with affection by everyone who knew her.

The Burg estate was given to the National Trust for Scotland in 1932 and Chrissie became custodian for them in 1936. She served in this capacity for 53 years and was highly regarded by the Trust. After being invited to the Royal Garden Party in Edinburgh she used to say the Queen (the late Queen Mother) was 'just like one of ourselves'. But it is doubtful if the Queen Mother could have made scones, cakes, oatcakes, butter and jam, or spin, dye and knit, as well as Chrissie! Many attempts to walk to the fossil tree used to end no further than Chrissie's kitchen where a 'blether' was enjoyed along with the tea. Near to the farmhouse are two memorials – one to Chrissie's brother, Duncan, and the other to Chrissie herself.

you are going. When you go down to the tree, do watch the tide as it is possible to get into serious difficulties.

In 1818, the geologist, John Mac-Culloch found the fossilized cast of a coniferous tree which grew 60 million years ago. At 40ft (12m) high and nearly five feet (1.5m) across it is regarded by many as the most interesting and impressive geological phenomenon on Mull. Unfortunately, it has been hacked about by unscrupulous people, but the National Trust for Scotland, who owns the peninsula, has tried to protect it.

For the less adventurous there is no need to go as far as the tree. Walking along the peninsula, especially if it is a good day, is reward enough for the view and wild life. Beyond the empty Burg farmhouse there is a **memorial to Daisy Cheape** on a rocky hill, or dun, near the sea.

Neolithic cairns and a number of duns or forts have been found on the Ardmeanach peninsula and there are the ruins of at least seven 19th- and 20th-century villages which housed a population of over 300. Beyond the farm, wild goats might be seen, whilst naturalists should keep a sharp eye open for rare wild flowers, birds and otters.

Returning to the converted church on the B8035, turn left and continue up through the glen. At the top there is the most wonderful view. It is possible to see over a dozen islands, from Iona on the far left, to Inch Kenneth, Ulva, Gometra, Little Colonsay, Staffa and the Treshnish islands in front, with Coll and Tiree on the horizon. If you are lucky enough to be here when the sun is setting it is a sight that you will remember for ever.

Walk to Mackinnon's cave

Down the hill from the viewpoint is a small road to the left. Mackinnon's cave is about a mile (1.6km) along here. Follow the track to the left around the farm of **Balemeanach** (*Ballymeenak*), through a gate and so to the cliff. The path winds down to the shore and a short scramble past a waterfall will bring you to the cave. **BUT CHECK THE TIDES**. The cave is only accessible at half tide and make sure it is falling to give yourself maximum time. Take a torch if you wish to go in as it is over 500ft (152m) deep.

The mystery is – does it go right through to Tiroran? One day, it is said, a piper called Mackinnon went in with a party who were determined to answer this question. Those above ground were following the sound of the pipes when they suddenly ceased. No-one ever came out alive except a dog which emerged, completely hairless, many days later from the hillside above Tiroran!

Gribun

The B8035 continues towards the **Gribun** (*Greebun*) **rocks** and in about three-quarters of a mile (1.2km) look out on the right for a particularly large boulder surrounded by a ruined wall. It is said that 150 years ago a newly married couple spent their honeymoon night here. The wind rose, the rain poured down and this huge rock crashed from the mountain above on to their cottage and there they still lie! On a fine summer day this catastrophe is hard to imagine but come here when a south-westerly gale is at full throttle; when the waterfalls are blown upwards making the mountain sides look as if

Gribun rocks

they are on fire and the spume from the waves rises like mist, and you can believe it! The road around the Gribun rocks requires care and patience, watching always for on-coming cars and being prepared to back. Watch, also, for small rocks and stones, which sometimes litter the road.

On the other side of the rocks the road runs on the south side of Loch na Keal. At one time there was a short but treacherous ferry crossing to Ulva from here. Possibly Thomas Campbell's poem, *Lord Ullin's Daughter*, was inspired by an incident in 1774 when a boat load of men became quarrelsome and started to fight. The boat sank with the loss of all eight passengers.

Ben More

The most usual path taken up **Ben More** starts by the cottage of **Dhiseig** (*Geeshug*). As the only Munro on Mull (over 3000ft [914m]) this mountain attracts many climbers or walkers. It is a slow, steady slog for the first 2000ft (610m), then the last part follows cairns along a broad ridge and up a sharp

---

Witch's home

Loch Ba is one of Mull's fresh water lochs with, near the Knock end, a crannog. Loch Ba was said to be the home of a famous witch who used to bathe every 100 years in its waters to renew her youthful appearance. But she had to do this early in the morning before any birds, beasts or humans were astir. For over a thousand years she was successful in remaining youthful and attractive. Then came the day when, as she made her way slowly down to the water, she disturbed a dog, which barked and instantly she perished.

ascent to the trig point. The views are extensive and spectacular in every direction even, on a clear day, extending as far as Northern Ireland.

Ben More was not a volcano but it is a minute part of the remains of one. It has curious magnetic properties as its basaltic rocks are rich in iron and cause compass bearings to be inaccurate and variable. Mist can come down very suddenly and it is possible to become completely disorientated so do take care and never set off without proper gear, emergency food and drink, a mobile phone and, most importantly, informing someone of your route. Ben More may look deceptively simple but, like mountains everywhere, it can be dangerous.

Walk along Loch Ba

In four miles (6.4km) the road turns inland, passes **Knock House** and farm and makes a sharp left bend. If you go straight ahead here and park the car you will find a track through a gate on the right, which goes along the shore of Loch Ba. It is a pleasant, easy walk which can be as long or short as you like. Just before the river, which is about two miles (3.2km) along, the old cattle drovers' road forks to the right. It climbs steeply over a pass and down the other side to the road through Glen More. Unless you are met here you will have to walk back – a great walk, but it is 10–12 miles (16–19km) in all and quite strenuous. If, instead of this, you cross the river and carry on for another two miles (3.2km) up

Coladoir River

Glenmore stories

The wildness and eeriness of Glen More, especially on gloomy winter nights with low cloud and mist making shifting shapes, has given rise to many stories. Some have historical foundations but have been added to and altered as the years have gone on until there are several versions, each one declared to be correct!

The Pedlar's Grave

In the winter of 1890 typhus came to Mull. A man fell ill at Kinloch and a friend from Bunessan, Mr Mitchell, went to nurse him. Mr Mitchell went back home, became ill himself and died. The Bunessan doctor had trouble finding someone to help put the poor man into his coffin as everyone was terrified of the illness. Eventually, John Jones a pedlar who lived in Bunessan, went to the doctor's aid. A day or two later he set out on his usual pedlar's round through Glen More. Meantime, Mr Mitchell's widow had been persuaded to return to Glasgow with her married daughter and grand-daughter. No-one would allow them in their boat so, against all medical advice, the three of them set out to walk the 25 miles (40km) to Craignure, hoping to get on a boat there. People in the houses of the Glen were afraid of catching typhus and left food out rather than take the travellers in.

The first night they slept out, huddled together, and the next day they overtook John Jones. Once at Craignure the Mitchell family were not allowed into the Inn but an old boat was upturned and made as comfortable a shelter as possible whilst they waited to take passage for Glasgow. That day Dr MacCallum from Salen was told that the pedlar's body had been found in the Glen. John Jones' death certificate said that he had died from exposure and money was collected for his widow, left alone in Bunessan. Years later this spot was selected to be called the 'Pedlar's Pool' and a small cairn was erected in memory of 'Jack Jones, the Pedlar'.

Missing butter

Halfway up the long hill in the Glen, is one of the inhabited houses. It was near here that Ewen of the Little Head, a son of the Chief of Lochbuie, fought his father for possession of land. The day before the battle Ewen met a fairy woman washing blood-stained clothes in a burn and singing a strange song. When Ewen asked how he would fare the next day she replied, 'Tomorrow, if there is butter on your breakfast table you will win. But if you have to ask for it, you will lose.' The next day, to Ewen's horror, there was no butter. Ewen and his men fought bravely but they were doomed. In a final gallop down the hill a claymore sliced off Ewen's head and his black horse raced on for several miles with his headless body still in the saddle. He finally fell and, on a black night you might feel the wind of his passing or even hear the groans and clash of battle around you!

Loch Ba, you will reach Glen Cannel with its ruined farmhouse and tiny burial ground.

Gruline

A mile beyond Loch Ba is the Gruline area where there are several things of interest. **Macquarie's Mausoleum** is signposted to the right with, incidentally, an incorrect spelling of the gentleman's name. The Mausoleum is maintained by the National Trust for Scotland on behalf of the National Trust of Australia (New South Wales). It is a plain, gable-ended building within a grassy enclosure, with a marble panel at one end commemorating Major General Lachlan Macquarie, Governor of New South Wales from 1810 to 1822, and his family.

The Episcopal church was built in 1873, financed by two of the local landowners. At its consecration by the Bishop of Argyll and the Isles, over 100 people were present. There are several memorial windows, the one opposite the door being a Kempe window. Kempe's trademark was a wheatsheaf and in this window there is a wheatsheaf with a tower superimposed on it. This indicates that his cousin, Walter Tower, was responsible for the work. The window is in memory of Frederic Jameson Elles who, in 1911 when he was 12, was drowned in Loch Frisa. The ashes of Frederic's mother, who died in 1966 at the age of 93, are buried in the graveyard opposite this window, beside those of her beloved son.

Opposite the drive up to the privately owned **Gruline House** is a building which once was the school. It was built in 1916 to replace one nearby which had been burnt down, and provided excellent education until the late 1960s. There was also a post office nearby which sold lemonade, biscuits, cigarettes and sweets to cater for the people who lived in the area, most of whom worked either in the Big House or on the Home Farm. From here it is about 3 miles (4.8km) back to Salen.

Father of Australia

Lachlan Macquarie (this is how he signed his name) was a crofter's son, born on Ulva in 1761. He served in the army and by 1800 had become a Major. Whilst in India he married Jane Jarvis but was widowed after only three years. His second wife was Elizabeth Henrietta Campbell. Two years after his second marriage Macquarie succeeded Captain Bligh as Governor of New South Wales, which post he held until 1822 when he, his wife, his 8-year-old son, his Indian servant, George, and his wife, returned to England.

Lachlan Macquarie died in London in 1824. Macquarie is sometimes referred to as 'The Father of Australia' as, during his tenure the backward, rough and primitive penal colony became the thriving embryo town of Sydney. Local people on Mull used to call the Mausoleum 'The Blackman's Tomb' because it was thought that George was buried there as well. Very few would pass it after dark and there have been reports of ghostly manifestations in the vicinity of the Mausoleum!

4. Brolas and the Ross of Mull

Loch Scridain

Kinloch

The road through Glen More joins the A849 near **Kinloch** and runs beside **Loch Scridain** (*Screetun*) down to Fionnphort (*Finafut*). Along all its 20 or so miles (32km) the views across the loch to the Ardmeanach peninsula are varied and magnificent. As there is no alternative you will have to return along the same route but this is no hardship as you will then be looking into the heart of Mull where great mountains stand guard at the entrance to the Glen.

Carsaig

Beyond **Pennyghael school**, now a Community Centre, is a turning to **Carsaig**. Although this is a no through road it is well worth going along the four miles (6.4km). From the cattle grid at the top of the hill, stop and look at the view before tackling the descent, which is very steep and narrow – take it carefully. Some distance down there is a telephone box on the left with, close beside it, a waterfall in full spate! This appeared in the original version of the film *I Know Where I'm Going*, some of which was shot in the Carsaig area and some in the Western Isles Hotel in Tobermory.

Inniemore Lodge-Studios occupies a spectacular position down here. It was established as a School of Painting in 1967 and painters came from far afield to attend courses run by qualified tutors. The house sleeps

In some ways Brolas and the Ross, or the south-western part of Mull, is different from the north and central parts. Physically it is further from the mainland ferries and, until the road through Glen More was improved, lack of access was a barrier which almost divided Mull into two parts. Even the Gaelic spoken used to have slight differences. Scenically, the Ross has no high mountains but there are dramatic cliffs along its southern coastline with wonderful bays and beaches of white sand. The northern coastline is less grand but has columnar rock formations similar to those on Staffa though smaller.

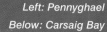

up to 12 and is surrounded by its own grounds. Self-catering accommodation is also available.

It is difficult to stop on the way down, but the views out to Jura, Islay and Colonsay and to the towering cliffs to the west, are dramatic. Down below, if you can glimpse it, is **Carsaig House,** once the home of 'Squire' Cheape of Bentley.

The Cheape family owned estates at Bentley in Worcestershire and on Mull. Colonel Cheape's wife had inherited the title of 'The Squire' when her father died and she was known by this name, even on Mull. The Squire was good to those less fortunate than herself and was much loved, being a familiar sight in her skirt of Maclean tartan as she drove her carriage around the island. At her death in 1919, of her six children only two were still alive. Two daughters had been drowned (one in Loch Scridain) and two sons were killed in WWI. On Mull she is still remembered, nearly 100 years after her death, by older people who have heard stories about her.

Walks at Carsaig

There are walks to east and west from Carsaig pier. That to the east can be continued to Lochbuie and, if long and muddy at the beginning, is fairly easy, except for the middle section. In spring the primroses and other wild flowers turn the area into a paradise.

The walk to the west is one of the most spectacular in the south of the

---

Devil's work

It is said that Loch Scridain was formed when St Columba and the Devil were arguing on top of Ben More. St Columba won and tossed the Devil over a precipice. At each bounce down the mountainside ledges appeared and his final fearsome fall created the loch!

island but it is also one of the most difficult and only for good walkers, properly equipped. It crosses the foot of soaring cliffs which reach 900ft (274m) and occasionally crumble in dangerous rock falls. Scrambling among the boulders is tiring, needing care and sure footedness.

About 2 miles (3.2km) along there is a gap in the great cliff wall where a steep grassy slope leads to the top. Here, at the bottom, is the **Nun's Cave** where it is said that nuns driven from Iona took refuge. Undoubtedly there are many crosses and symbols incised on the walls, some of which are thought to be early Christian. Amongst them are masons' marks, a sailing ship and the date 1633. Another two miles (3.2km) further on is the amazing natural phenomenon known as the Carsaig Arches. These were once caves which have gradually been eroded to form a dark, mysterious tunnel 140ft (43m) long and also a tall, graceful pile topped by a finger of rock.

The **Carsaig Arches** are on the promontory of **Malcolm's Point**, at a place known as **Gorrie's Leap**. It was here that a relation of Maclaine of Lochbuie took terrible revenge for savage punishment inflicted upon him. Seizing a Maclaine baby he succeeded in reaching this cliff where he leapt to his death with the child in his arms.

Returning to the A849 continue towards Fionnphort. Shortly, on the right near a church, now a private house, can be seen an old cross. It is surrounded by trees and bracken but a gap has been cut so that it can be seen from the road, but perhaps more easily when travelling in the opposite direction. The cross was erected to the memory of the famous Beaton family of doctors and bears the date 1582.

Scoor

In another 8–9 miles (13–14.5km), just before reaching Bunessan, there is a turning to **Scoor**. Up here, far from any sounds save those of the wind and birds, are the ruins of the church of **Kilvickeon** (*Kilvikuan*) standing near **Loch Assapol**. This church was one of seven mediaeval chapels on Mull and dates to the 13th century. Its name means church of the son of Eoghan (Uan), who was a relation of Columba. It was probably in use for well over 500 years with, of course, many alterations and additions during this time. As well as the local stone used, see if you can spot the fertility symbol carved in sandstone. This is very unusual for a Scottish church. There are grave slabs, table tombs and headstones within and around the ruin, some of them very old indeed.

If you continue beyond this, up to the farm of Scoor and then by foot, you will find magnificent white sandy beaches. To the west is a cave 50ft (15m) deep, on the walls of which are curious depressions and markings similar to those in the Nun's cave. There are many wonderful walks across the moorland around here. There are deserted villages where once over 300 people lived, secret coves where wet sand glints a startling silver, and deer, eagles and wild goats might be seen with the backdrop of a panorama of islands floating in an azure sea.

One of the deserted villages is **Shiaba** (*Sheeaba*). Here are the remains of buildings and enclosures where in 1841, 126 people lived in 22 cottages. By 1881 two people remained, too old and ill to move. From 1845 until 1870 the Duke of Argyll had appointed a factor to look after the Ross of Mull property. This man, John Campbell, raised rents, deprived people of their pasture land and forcibly removed them from their cottages, not only in Shiaba, but throughout the area. The years of his cruelty and harshness aroused ill feeling and hatred that still reverberates today in the memories of Ross people.

Bunessan

Just before entering Bunessan you will see the ruins of a mill on the right. This was built in the 18th century for grinding oatmeal that would first have been roasted over a peat fire. A miller was a vitally important and respected member of every community and needed to be an engineer and joiner as well as skilled in controlling the water needed to operate his mill. This was last in use at the start of the 20th century.

In 1879 thieves stole one and a half stones (9.5kg) of meal from this mill by prising out a bar and entering through a window on the south side. Although other bags of meal stood inside they only took a small amount but even this was worth 4/6d (about 23p), a fair sum for those days.

The village of **Bunessan** has shops, a hotel, tearoom and post office, but no petrol – that is another few miles further on. As you enter the village, the road to the right leads to **Ardtun** which is famous for its 54 million-year-old fossilised leaf beds composed of layer upon layer of leaves which fell into an ancient lake.

In World War II the Royal Navy were in Bunessan. They renovated the jetty and built the 'new' piece of road which runs out of the village by the sea, past a small building which houses the **Ross of Mull Historical Centre.** Although small, this contains a mass of information about the geology, flora, fauna, social history and genealogy of the Ross. Plans are afoot for the Centre to move into bigger buildings. As you go up the hill, look for a left turn to **Uisken** (*Ushken*) where there is a beautiful sandy beach at **Ardalanish**. Right by the beach are two standing stones (one now lying down!) and, further to the west, one of the most wonderfully situated ancient rock fortresses on Mull.

At Ardalanish is an organic farm where Highland cattle and Hebridean sheep are kept. The owners of this farm have great plans for the future and you are most welcome to visit and see what is going on – maybe tanning from their own animal skins or weaving from their own wool.

Fionnphort

The Ross of Mull has long been famous for its pink granite, which in a sinking summer sun, makes parts of the landscape glow as if lit from within. The granite has been quarried from several places around **Fionnphort**. One of these was at a bay called **Camus Tuath** and a short walk across the moor from the A849 brings you to the old buildings near the shore. The quarry is across the bay where remains of the workings can still be seen. In 1844 blocks from here were used to build Skerryvore lighthouse, 10 miles (16km) south-west of Tiree.

Even finer granite was obtained from the **Tormore quarry** nearer to Fionnphort. Walk up the track past Bruach Mor going towards the north coast and up the hill are the old workings, originally opened in 1831. After some years they closed, were reopened towards the end of the 20th century, only to be abandoned again. Huge blocks of cut granite lie about and drill holes can still be seen, plus the long railway track leading down to the pier. This distinctive stone, which polishes to a warm, rich pinky-red sheen, was once exported all over the world, including America and China. In Britain it has been used in many places such as the Albert Memorial, Jamaica Bridge in Glasgow and Blackfriars Bridge in London.

Kintra

About a mile before the track to this quarry there is a turning which goes to **Kintra**, a tiny place set around a bay. It was founded in the 1770s by the 5th Duke of Argyll in an attempt to provide an income for himself and his tenants through fishing. The 12 crofts were inhabited but the distance from mainland markets meant that the scheme foundered. The nearby granite quarries provided some employment for the villagers and at one time there were three shops. However, the quarries closed, families emigrated and some were evicted. The village gradually became depopulated until, in the 1920s, there were only two people left. Now, the village is gradually coming back to life, an encouraging sight. Whilst down here, see if you can find the fairy footprint in the rocks at the east side of the bay.

The A849 ends at Fionnphort by the ferry for Iona. There are shops, a restaurant and accommodation. A turning to the left leads to the **Columba Centre** where there is an exhibition about St Columba and a large car park. This road continues past the Centre, first to the farm of **Fidden** (*Feejun*) and then to **Knockvologan** where it finishes. The beaches around Fidden are of white sand, a temptingly beautiful area for tents and caravans. You can walk for miles here, even across to the **island of Erraid** if the tide is right and you have permission, or across the moorland, absorbing the peace and natural beauty around you.

At Knockvologan, a gate across the road near a bungalow by some farm buildings, is as far as you can go by car. If you can park here you will find a notice on the side of the barn telling you about the area, called **Tireragan** (*Chireregan*), which is of great conservation importance. Since 1994 it has been managed by Highland Renewal, a local charity devoted to the regeneration of woodlands and other habitats, as well as to education and research.

Several walks, of varying lengths, have been waymarked by different colours. One leads to an abandoned village where 100 people used to live and another goes to a remote and beautiful beach, which you will find difficult to leave at the end of the day. But, if you chose to walk on along the road, through the gate, please keep dogs on a lead. You will find your way down to other stunning beaches where you can walk, bathe perhaps, or just sit and enjoy the solitude.

5. Off Shore Islands

Ulva and Gometra

Ulva can be reached from Mull by a five-minute ride in an open boat. It is linked to Gometra, about five miles (8km) distant, by a causeway or bridge. Both islands are privately owned and there is a charge for the ferry, which is for pedestrians and cyclists only.

Once over the Sound of Ulva you step into a different existence where there are no tarmac roads, no traffic noises or smells, no hustle, no bustle. You can take your time to enjoy the walks, the signs of earlier inhabitants, the plant life – some of it rare – the birds and the animals. Or you can just amble to a picnic spot and allow the peace to soak right into your bones whilst letting your senses become attuned to the quietness.

History of the islands

Ulva and Gometra have been in-habited for centuries. Archaeologists studying the floor of one of the caves on the south side of Ulva have found remains that suggest it was in use as a dwelling place thousands of years ago. Two standing stones remain from four thousand years later, and there are forts and duns which indicate the presence of people later still. Remains of cottages, mills, schools and graveyards bring us up to the last two centuries. During the 19th century Ulva supported 16 crofting communities with over 600 inhabitants, whilst on Gometra there were 200 people and a separate school,

Guillemots on the Harp Rock, Lunga

which did not close until 1938.

Over the centuries the two islands have seldom had the same owner. Ulva was owned by the clan MacQuarrie for 500 years until the late 18th century. In 1773 Johnson and Boswell landed there in the dark and were told by their MacQuarrie host that there was nothing worth seeing on the island. By this he probably meant that there were no historic monuments of note.

At the end of the 18th century Ulva came into the possession of the Macdonald family of Boisdale. Ranald Macdonald also acquired Gometra in 1807 and his mother and two sisters lived there for a number of years. Meanwhile, everyone of any impor-tance called, usually on their way to Staffa. Mrs Murray stayed for a month in 1800 and enjoyed the benefits of a grand new house that had been built.

Explorer's history

The paternal grandparents of David Livingstone, the explorer, were respected crofters on Ulva in the 18th century. They went through a lean time and were forced to spend some months living in a cave on the south side of the island. The Livingstone family eventually moved to the mainland and, in 1813, David was born in Blantyre.

Ranald Macdonald entertained his guests royally, often meeting them in his boat, adorned with flags, and his piper, Archibald MacArthur, playing for them. Macdonald managed his property well, apparently liked by his tenants, and considered humane and attentive to their needs. But, in 1817 he faced bankruptcy and ruin. The islands had to be sold.

It was not until 1826 that the next purchaser came to Ulva. This was Colonel Charles Macquarie, brother of Lachlan Macquarie of New South Wales fame. The brothers were distantly related to the chief of the island and Charles, when he had a little capital, but not sufficient to prevent heavy debts accumulating, had a fancy to buy his childhood home. His tenure lasted only ten years. He died in 1835 and the islands had to be sold to pay his debts. The next proprietor was FW Clark, a lawyer from Stirling.

During the late 18th and early 19th centuries kelp burning had been the principal industry on the two islands. By the end of the Napoleonic Wars this was no longer profitable. Shortly afterwards, disastrous harvests and the potato blight ruined the crofters' main source of food. According to his own accounts, Francis William Clark, tried to provide work to relieve the resultant starvation and distress but he found it impossible. He felt he had no alternative but to reduce the population. Many were forced to emigrate to America, Australia and other parts of the world and also to parts of Mull. FW Clark seems to have cleared crofters off his island with little sympathy. Many years later an old man spoke of the cruelty that he had witnessed as families were removed and their cottages razed to the ground. At his death in 1887 Clark was a hated man and his memory still lingers as a bitter taste in the mouth.

After being in the Clark family for 110 years Ulva and Gometra were bought by Lady Congleton in 1945 and Ulva has remained in her family ever since although Gometra, once again, has a separate owner. In 1950 the big house was burnt down during renovations and the present house was built. The population has steadily declined

Beatrix Potter

Caroline Hutton was a distant cousin of Beatrix Potter. Caroline married FW Clark (the third one of that name) who had inherited Ulva, and was 12 years her senior. At the age of 42, in 1912, Caroline gave birth to the fourth generation of Clarks to be associated with Ulva. Whilst Caroline's child was still a baby Beatrix wrote *The Tale of Mr Tod* and dedicated it to William Francis of Ulva. Caroline and Beatrix were great friends and corresponded frequently.

but the island has recently taken on a new lease of life with the opening of a Visitor Centre, Sheila's Cottage Exhibition and the tearoom.

Ulva

The **Boathouse Visitor's Centre** and **Sheila's Cottage** are near the landing place The display upstairs in the former will give you an excellent idea of the island's history and the tearoom beneath provides home made snacks and lunches. Sheila's Cottage also contains exhibits of interest. Sheila was a dairymaid who lived in this cottage until the 1950s.

Continue along the rough track past the cottage and you can take your pick from a number of walks, all well signposted. One goes to the church and farm, another goes through woodland to the shore, another to *Livingstone's cave* and fine basalt columns that rival those of Staffa. Or, further away are the ruins of **Ormaig** with its mill, **Kilvekewen** and the graveyard or, if you are a good walker, you can go the five miles (8km) right down to Gometra. On the other hand, you may wish to strike out on your own but, wherever you go, please remember that the island is a working farm and dogs must be kept on a lead.

The church and manse were both designed by Thomas Telford. The last minister resident on Ulva left in 1929. The interior of the church was much altered during the 1950s and the rather unusual pulpit was restored. In recent years well-attended services have been held in the church at Easter, Harvest and Christmas and it has proved to be a popular and unusual venue for christenings and weddings. The manse is a private house.

High on a rather prominent hill on Ulva can be seen a walled enclosure. This is a burial ground and inside are monuments to the Clark family. The memorial is built on the site of an ancient fort and can only be reached after a difficult scramble. It is said that during its construction a cart, which was bringing one of the heavy slabs, became stuck so firmly in the boggy ground that it had to be unloaded in order to move it. The horse and cart were released but the slab was too heavy to lift and reload. It lies to this day, somewhere on the hillside buried beneath the bracken and undergrowth, slowly sinking into the bog.

Both Ulva and Gometra are a paradise for naturalists. No-one can guarantee what you will see, let alone be able to identify, but deer, hares, stoats, otters and seals are relatively common. Well over 100 different birds have been sighted, from the commoner ones to less common species such as petrels, corncrakes, white tailed eagles and sparrow hawks. The trees and flowers to be found run into the hundreds and then there are the ferns and fungi! A visit to Ulva and down the five-mile track to Gometra if you have time, is likely to be full of interest for everyone. Prepare to relax and go quietly, respecting and absorbing the wild life and history around you.

Inch Kenneth

Inch Kenneth is a privately owned island and it is not possible to visit except by permission of the owners. It has an interesting history. At one time it was used by the monks of Iona as their granary and in the 15th and 16th century it was in the hands of the Augustinian Nuns of Iona. From then on there were various owners including Macleans, MacDonalds, Clarks of Ulva, the Lows and the Redesdales.

Inch Kenneth is shaped rather like a woeful dog with its tail down, the 'tail' being a series of hillocks known as 'humpies'. Its geological composition is different from that of Mull and the 130 acres (53ha) are extremely fertile, in the past growing, excellent crops and vegetables.

History

Its name is said to derive from St Cainnech, a contemporary of Columba, and on the island there are the ruins of a 13th-century church, which possibly replaced a wooden one of Cainnech, or Kenneth's, time. The mediaeval building would have been used as a parish church and there is a double lancet window in the ruins of the east wall. The base of the altar can still be seen, along with funerary monuments and carved stones dating from mediaeval times to the 18th century. They are worn and weathered and mostly commemorate Macleans but it is said that Kings of Scotland and Ireland were sometimes buried here if prolonged storms prevented passage to Iona.

Inch Kenneth fell within the Brolas section of the Duart estate and was taken by the Campbell's of Argyll in payment of the Duart debts. Hector Maclean of Brolas leased the island back

---

The Mitford sisters

The Redesdales were a brilliant, eccentric family of six daughters (the Mitford sisters) and one son. Nancy, the eldest, lived in Paris. She used to call travelling to Inch Kenneth the worst journey in the world but, once there, she thought it the most beautiful place in the world. Diana Mitford first married Bryan Guinness and then Oswald Mosley. Diana often visited the island but Mosley always stayed on Mull in a house opposite the island. Maybe he did not like small boats!

Jessica, 'Decca', was the third daughter. She wrote *The American Way of Death* whilst on Inch Kenneth. Pamela was the fifth daughter and the most 'normal'. She became the Honourable Mrs Jackson and eventually lived in a small village in the Cotswolds. The youngest daughter was Deborah who married the Duke of Devonshire. Tom, the only son was killed in World War II, fighting the Japanese in Burma.

Unity was the fourth daughter. She was besotted by Hitler and, on the declaration of war, was so devastated that she shot herself in the head. The bullet lodged in her brain but did not kill her and she was rushed to a clinic. Hitler rang often to ask how she was and, eventually, arranged for her return to England via Switzerland, but she was not allowed to go back to Inch Kenneth until 1944, because it lay in a restricted area. The brain damage had changed her personality completely but she and her mother lived on the island until, in 1948 Unity became ill with meningitis brought on by the old wound. She died in Oban Hospital in May 1948.

from the Duke of Argyll and shored up the walls of the ancient chapel, as well as building himself a small cottage and byres.

Sir Allan Maclean of Duart and Brolas was the next owner and, in October 1773 Johnson and Boswell landed during their grand tour in the Highlands. Their host was Sir Allan, who had 'a commodious habitation' – in fact, slightly superior cottages. But the travellers were greatly impressed by the manners and conversation of their host and his two daughters, and by the pile of newspapers which Johnson thoroughly enjoyed reading. Once again, the island had to be sold to pay debts, and it was bought by Charles Maclean of Drimnin, who had married one of Sir Allan's daughters.

Early in the 19th century Inch Kenneth was bought by Colonel Robert Macdonald. It was he who had a new house built. This was in a poor state by the time Walter Scott came some years later. By the middle of the 19th century the Clarks of Ulva owned the island but they sold it, towards the end of the century, to the Malloch family. In the early 1920s it came into the possession of Mary Low who added to and altered the house during her years there.

The next owners made several more alterations to the house, including adding a bow front and building a chapel on the top floor. Just before World War II Lord Redesdale acquired Inch Kenneth and it belonged to the family until it was bought by Dr and Mrs Barlow in the 1960s.

During the time of the Low family, annual sports and a dance were held

View from Lunga (Treshnish Isles) with the Dutchman's Cap (right and the Harp Rock (centre)

on the island. Sometimes the weather meant that large numbers of people had to spend an unexpected night there, either in the farmhouse or the big house. One of the Low children remembered an old woman saying that, as a youngster she had seen a man dressed in 18th-century clothes walking near the house – maybe it was the ghost of one of the Maclean owners of the past!

Inch Kenneth has a wonderful beauty and charm. It is full of bird life, delightful flowers and fascinating history. No wonder it has attracted people over the centuries. There is an ancient cairn and a standing stone; a Viking hoard, including coins and bangles, has been unearthed and, in the 1950s, bottles of whisky were found secreted in niches all over the island! These might have been left from the time when a previous owner's wife, who was an alcoholic, lived there. If one can receive permission, it is a great place to spend a day, picnic in one of the tiny sheltered coves and soak up the unspoilt tranquillity.

Treshnish Islands

These islands can be seen as you look out to sea from the western side of Mull. They lie in a line from south-west to north-east, four miles (6.4km) west of Gometra. Their strange shapes are distinctive against the sky as they sail eternally into the sunset – even Queen Victoria once made a simple sketch of them. From the south the Dutchman's Cap, Lunga, Fladda, Cairnburgh Mor and Cairnburgh Beg are the most obvious, with several smaller islets discernable between Lunga and Fladda. Landing on them is difficult but not impossible and there are several boat trips to Lunga. They are a sanctuary for a wide variety of sea birds and seals and at one time they were used to pasture sheep and cattle as they grow lush grass fertilized by the vast quantities of sea bird droppings. Wild flowers grow in abundance and they are now a special area of conservation.

The **Dutchman's Cap**, or **Bac Mor**, is connected by a causeway to its smaller neighbour, **Bac Beag**. Bac Mor actually looks more like a Mexican sombrero or even a witch's hat as it has a flat brim with a hill in the middle as the crown. The brim would once have been below sea level with only the crown sticking out above the waves. There were ruins of cottages on the island and it is said that at the bottom of a deep hollow there is a tunnel leading to the cliffs on the western side.

Lunga is the island that looks like a battleship and it is the most visited. On the western side is a rocky stack separated from the main island by about 20ft (6m). The seaward side of this stack is a sheer rock face nearly 150ft (46m) high. In spring it is a most impressive sight as the whole rock is a seething, raucous mass of birds – kittiwakes, guillemots, gulls, fulmars – all jostling and fighting to keep possession of their tiny space. Lunga itself is covered with puffins, a delightful clown of a bird with its Charlie Chaplin feet and bright beak, usually full of neatly packed sand eels for its chicks. If you happen to have your own feet near a burrow it will eye you from close range with a glare which clearly says 'Do you mind!' Having delivered the meal it will pop up again, launch into space and soar with unexpected grace, seeking more food far out to sea where it spends the rest of the year. As many as 52 different species of bird have been seen on Lunga.

The two **Cairnburgh islands** lie in a strategic position commanding one of the sea approaches to the Inner Hebrides. An ancient fort stood on the larger island and, it is said, that the records of Iona Abbey were sent here for safe keeping but subsequently lost. Later, a chapel, castle and fortifications were built on the ruins of the fort. These two islands have seen stirring events and battles over the years, particularly during the 17th century when the Macleans and Campbells fought for supremacy. The forts were garrisoned as recently as the 18th century.

An expedition to these beautiful islands often forms the highlight of a visitor's tour to this part of the western isles.

Erraid

The island of **Erraid** lies off the south-western tip of the Ross of Mull. For nearly 30 years it has been privately owned. It is about one mile (1.6m) square and it is possible to walk across to it at a very low tide but watch out – the tide comes in from both direc-

Kelp

Kelp is a substance obtained from *laminaria* seaweed. It was found that the alkaline ash from burning the weed was useful in making glass, soap and bleaching agents. The Napoleonic Wars stopped the importing of this ash and, as a result, the price rose dramatically. It fell equally dramatically when normal trade was resumed after the war. The processes of collecting, drying and burning the seaweed were labour intensive, unpleasant and back-breaking. Whilst there was money to be made, landlords had encouraged crofters on to their land and the population on Ulva and Gometra had risen. The disastrous fall in price meant that these crofters, who had been reliant on the work, no longer had paid employment and their landlords also lost much of their income. In common with many places in Scotland, the economy of Ulva and Gometra collapsed.

tions and you can get caught.

Seeing the quietness of the island now, it is hard to imagine that it was once the scene of great industry, noise and activity. In the 19th century Erraid was the base for the building of **Dhuheartach** (*Duersta*) **lighthouse** 15 miles out in the Atlantic on St John's rock. This lighthouse was masterminded by one of the Stevenson family who produced several generations of great engineers. Thomas was responsible for Dhuheartach. He was Robert Louis Stevenson's father and the 20-year-old author spent three weeks on Erraid in 1870 when work had begun. He described the scene vividly as huge cranes sprouted from the landscape, gigantic blocks of granite were cut and shaped and the air was full of the din of machinery and the shouts of men. Bothies were built to house the workers and, on a Sunday when all was still and peaceful, one of these was used for worship.

For nearly 100 years Erraid was the shore station for the lighthouse keepers for both Dhuheartach and Skerryvore. The latter had been erected in the 1840s by an uncle of Robert Louis Stevenson. The row of houses, which is still there,

was built for the wives and families of the keepers and, for much of that time, they had their own school.

In 1977 Erraid was purchased by a Dutchman who leased it to the **Findhorn Community**, which had been founded in 1962 and grown into a dynamic collective with its headquarters near Inverness. The community on Erraid grows organic produce, tries to live in harmony with nature and conducts a sustainable lifestyle. All the year round they run educational programmes for families and visitors who join in their workshops, circle dancing, BBQs and other activities. Everyone is welcome whether for a holiday, to work or merely to meditate and appreciate the beauty of the island.

Kidnapped

Robert Louis Stevenson used Erraid in one of his most famous stories. David Balfour, the hero of *Kidnapped*, was cast away here after his captivity on the Covenant. He dragged himself ashore and began his flight through mountains, bog and heather as he crossed Erraid and then Mull.

6. Iona

The island of Iona lies off the south-western tip of Mull. It is reached by a short ferry ride from Fionnphort, which lies 35 miles (56km) from Craignure. Buses do operate between these, but only two or three times a day. It is not possible to take a vehicle over to Iona without authorisation but bicycles are permitted and there is free parking at the Columba Centre at Fionnphort. The ferries are frequent in summer but less so in winter, particularly on Sundays, and they can be disrupted due to inclement weather. There are two hotels, Bishops House, bed and breakfast accommodation, a Hostel, two general stores and a post office as well as craft shops and a restaurant.

Book of Kells

This was written around 800 AD, probably begun on Iona but finished in the Abbey of Kells in Ireland. It has been described as 'the work not of men but of angels' and is acknowledged to be one of the most wondrous books in the world. It is written on fine vellum, for which the skin of 200 calves was used, in insular majuscule script and consists of the Latin text of the four gospels with prefaces, summaries and canon tables. Of its 680 pages only two are without decorative illuminations. And what illuminations! Some take up a whole page, others form capital letters and others appear as marginal extras with occasional humorous sketches.

Ten colours were used, each having to be ground and mixed. The ingredients for these must have been imported from as far away as Asia. The brown ink used for the text was made from crushed oak apples. Some of the decorations are so minute that they must be magnified ten times to see the exact and fine detail. It is thought that there were four master painters and calligraphers with, possibly, five apprentices to do the preparation and occasional minor pieces. The original has been in the library of Trinity College, Dublin since 1661.

St Columba

Columba and his 12 followers arrived on Iona in 563 AD, possibly at a little bay at the south end which is still called the **Bay of the Coracle**. Tradition says, that having made sure that the coast of Ireland was not visible from the top of the cliffs, they walked across the island and founded their settlement, just north of where the present Abbey lies. The earliest huts were small and simple, made of wattle and daub as there were still many trees to provide the material. As time passed the monks built a small church, a guest house, a refectory, a mill and sleeping quarters which were all enclosed by an earthwork or vallum. Evidence of post holes and references to fetching reeds from Mull, in ancient records seem to suggest that these buildings were made from wood and thatch.

Columba was a remarkable man – a man of Christ and a friend of people, a priest, a poet and a statesman. To him life was a unity – to pray was to work and to work was to pray. He and his followers influenced the agriculture, art, learning and politics of the day, as well as becoming the power house of Celtic Christianity which reached out, via his missionaries, to the northern Picts and as far as the north of England. They were experts and craftsmen of rare ability who not only cared for the souls of men but also excelled in activities such as wood carving, metalwork, building, healing, enamelling and, above all, in the art of illumination. Traces of workshops and a few fragments of their work have been unearthed by archaeologists.

The life the monks led was rigorous, labouring in the fields and on the sea, studying, transcribing and illuminating the scriptures. They also undertook long journeys over land and sea. Columba is said to have been responsible for founding anywhere between 50 and 300 churches as his influence spread far and wide. Iona itself became a place of pilgrimage and has remained so for over 1400 years. Columba died, close to his Abbey, in 597 at the age of 77.

Most people immediately associate Iona with St Columba and the Abbey. But this small island packs more archaeological, religious and social history into its six square miles (15.5sqm) than many 20 times its size, to say nothing of its stunning natural history. Anyone who sees Iona on a sunny summer day cannot fail to be transfixed by its magical radiance. On a dull day there is something about the luminous quality of the light which enhances even the most sombre shades. Many who visit feel a magnetic attraction and return time and time again.

Geology

It is not only for its ecclesiastical history that Iona is famous. There is great fascination for the geologist as some of the rocks belong to the oldest geological formations known. Much of the central and western part is composed of Lewisian gneiss, probably 1500 million years old, whilst the eastern side contains Torridonian sediments. At the south-eastern tip is a marble quarry where fine-grained greenish rocks occur which can be quarried in huge blocks, or smaller pieces might break off naturally and become weathered by the action of the sea. Pebbles of wondrous serpentine beauty varying from dark green to a light yellowish shade can be found on the beaches. Amongst the rocks on Iona is some of the Lower Old Red Sandstone granite found in abundance in the Ross of Mull. Over millions of years the sea level has risen and fallen, there have been ice ages and volcanic activity whilst Atlantic storms and gales have battered the land – as a result, Iona has the raised beaches, cliffs, dykes, hillocks and shell beaches of today. Unlike Mull, there is no peat and only one shallow loch, which meant that, at one time, it had to rely on springs for drinking water.

History

Some authorities believe that, many centuries before Christ, Iona was a focus of Druid worship. Years ago, in an ancient burial ground south-west of the present village, several skulls were found, which were thought to be of great antiquity. But, as the Gaelic for Druid (Druidneach) and sculptors (Druineach) are very similar, perhaps some mistake has occurred in the past. It is certain that Iron Age man was on the island as there are the remains of a fort on the western shore.

The monastery, which Columba founded, was raided and plundered several times by the Vikings. In 806, 68 monks were murdered. For a time those remaining retreated to Ireland but, later, a new monastery was built on Iona, only to fall prey to the Danes in the 10th century. More monks were murdered but, in spite of these repeated attacks, Iona survived as a place of pilgrimage and holiness, although the monks retreated and the buildings gradually fell into ruins.

By 1074 Queen Margaret, wife of Malcolm III, had had the monastery restored and many of the most important people of Scotland and Ireland were buried in the graveyard near the Abbey. Some of the grave slabs from these early burials have been found. However, by the 12th century all had again become ruinous. Eventually Reginald, Lord of the Isles, came to possess Iona. The monastery was rebuilt in 1203 and became the home of the 'Black Monks', or Benedictines. St Oran's Chapel in the graveyard by the Abbey, was probably built by Reginald, or his father, Somerled, as a family burial chamber. Also at this time, the nunnery was built and Beatrice, Reginald's sister, was installed as the first Prioress. The ruins of this nunnery are amongst the best in Europe.

The fortunes of Abbey and Convent ebbed and flowed for the next 300 years. For a short time at the beginning of the 16th century Iona became a Cathedral when it was the seat of John, Bishop of the Isles but, at the Reformation in 1561 the Abbey and its buildings were dismantled. The ruins mouldered quietly away, some of the stones being used for walls, byres and cottages, weeds gradually covering the cloisters and walls. Where once had been the music and chanting of monks there was only the lowing of cattle and the cries of birds. Yet, there was a long established secular population on Iona, outside these ruins, and their life continued for the next 300 years.

In 1899, just before he died, George, 8th Duke of Argyll, who owned Iona by this time, gave the ruins to the Iona Cathedral Trust. Public subscriptions were sought and the church of the Abbey was restored between 1902 and 1910. Restoration of the other buildings was started under the inspiration of the Rev. George F Macleod, then a parish minister in Glasgow, who founded the Iona Community in 1938. This work was completed in the mid 1960s. In 1979 the whole island was bought by the Fraser Foundation and given to the nation under the care of the National Trust for Scotland. The Iona Cathedral Trust transferred the Abbey, Nunnery and Reilig Oran graveyard to the care of Historic Scotland in 2000.

Window, Iona Abbey

Around the Abbey

Slightly to the south of the Abbey is an ancient burial ground, **Reilig Odhrain** (Burial place of Oran). According to tradition Oran, one of Columba's disciples, was the first to die and was buried here, near their tiny church. But it is not known if this is true. However, over the next 500 years, as the fame of Iona grew and spread, this became a holy and venerated place. By the 16th century it was said that 48 Scottish Kings, including Duncan and Macbeth, four Irish Kings and seven Norwegian Kings were buried there in three chapel-like tombs. Chiefs of the Scottish Clans and, in more recent centuries, islanders themselves are also buried outside in the graveyard.

Street of the Dead

This is a cobbled street, part of it uncovered in 1962, which linked the burial ground with the Abbey. It may once have gone as far as the **Bay of Martyrs**, which is near the jetty. It was along here that coffins would have been carried on their way to Reilig Odhrain.

Above: Iona Abbey and (inset) interior of St Oran's Chapel

More recently still, American sailors who drowned nearby and the ex-Labour leader, John Smith, have found their resting place here. There are many old and fascinating grave slabs both in the graveyard and within the chapel.

The High Crosses

At one time there were many old crosses on Iona but some have vanished. There are now four that are of interest.

St Martin's: This is the original and was made from a single block of whinstone in the late eighth or early ninth century. The slots at the end of the arms once held wooden or granite extensions. Its carving is rich and beautiful and depicts the Virgin and Child, Old Testament scenes, decorative

Within the Abbey of St Columba

Inside the Abbey can be seen many traces of the expansion and reconstruction which has taken place since its foundation in the 12th century. For instance the nave has been widened, the choir roof altered and the floor level changed. Most of the choir and transepts are late 15th- or early 16th-century whilst the majority of the nave is early 20th-

Carved capitals, Iona Abbey

century. The oldest part is the east wall of the north transept, which dates back to the beginning of the 13th century. The wall here is very thick and there is a narrow passageway in it, above the windows, but its purpose is unknown. In this transept are the night stairs, which the monks used and the oak screen that was a gift from Queen Elizabeth in 1956.

The carved capitals on the south side of the choir represent mythical birds, beasts, biblical scenes and figures. There is an angel weighing souls and a very secular scene of a cow being stolen! High above on the west crossing arch a demonic gargoyle grimaces down as if in torment. In the south transept is a monument to the 8th Duke of Argyll and his third wife. The latter is buried there but the Duke was taken to the family vault at Kilmun on the mainland.

Some inscribed crosses can be made out on the wall nearby which were probably done at the consecration of the building. The altar table, of modern Iona marble, has a beautiful covering that was done in recent years. In front of the table are the effigies of two of the 15th-century abbots. Above, the clerestory windows show St Columba, St Bride and St Patrick and in the window on the south side is a model of an old curragh, similar to a coracle. In the stonework on each side of this window are a cat and a monkey, representing activity and contemplation, the two major occupations expected of a monk.

The cloisters are unusual in that they are placed on the north side of the church. Only two of the columns are original, the rest being beautiful modern carvings depicting birds, flowers and plants. The bronze sculpture in the middle was carved in 1959 by Joseph Lipchitz, a Lithuanian Jew. It symbolizes the 'Descent of the Spirit'. Above the east range was the monks' dormitory with the Chapter House beneath it, and to the north would have been the refectory.

intertwined serpents and prominent bosses.

St John's: The original was blown down so many times that it was removed to the museum behind the Abbey and an exact replica put in its place. Its decoration is so intricate that one can only marvel at the skill of the workmen.

St Matthew's: Only the base of this remains outside the Abbey. The rest is in the museum.

Maclean's: This is to be found beside the road leading up to the Abbey from the village. It is thought to be 15th-century, hewn out of schist. On the west side is a crucifix in the solid head and on the east side is rich, delicate carving of tracery and inter-leaved patterns. It has been suggested that the road originally ran on the other side of this cross.

The Nunnery

On the way from the ferry landing-place to the Abbey you can walk through the ruins of the **Nunnery**. The first Prioress in 1203 was Beatrice and the last was Anna in 1543. One of the most notable monuments in the nunnery was that belonging to Anna – her likeness was cut on the stone, an angel on each side supports her head and above is a mirror and a comb. A stone carved with seven figures is another relic, and a number of other stones beautifully carved with leaves and delicate tracery have been moved to the museum. The Nunnery cloister, with its church on the north, chapter house on the east and refectory on the south, can still be clearly seen. When the garden in the cloister was being made in 1923, three silver gilt spoons were found dating from the 13th century.

Scottish Colourists

These were a group of four Scottish artists – JD Ferguson, GL Hunter, SJ Peploe and F Cadell – who were greatly influenced by French painters such as Cézanne. They worked in the early 20th century – Cadell, for instance, first went to Iona in 1912 and Peploe in 1920 – and found the light and shades of Iona inspiring. They returned year after year and their paintings are much sought after nowadays.

The Iona Community

This is an ecumenical Christian community founded in 1938 by the Rev. George Macleod. The main function of the community is to seek ' new ways to touch the hearts of all'. The members work for social and political concerns, they explore new approaches to worship and have a strong ecumenical commitment. There are about 250 Members, over 1500 Associates and 1700 Friends who come from all over the world and from every background. They live in their local communities where they become involved in environmental issues, promote peace and justice, support the poor and exploited, and work for interdenominational understanding. There are three residential bases – Iona Abbey and the Macleod Centre on Iona, and Camas on the Ross of Mull. These are run by a resident group of 25, assisted by 30 or so volunteers from all over the world. Guests are welcome to stay, either in the living quarters of the Community or in the Macleod Centre, and join

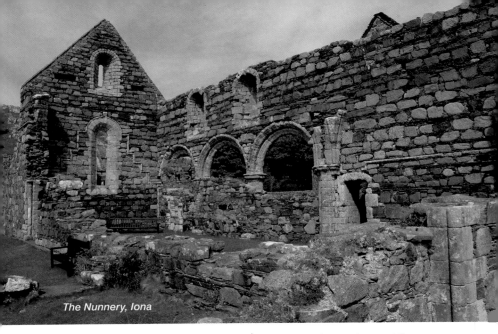

The Nunnery, Iona

the worship, discussion and recreation. The Community has its administrative headquarters in Glasgow.

The north end of Iona

In summer Iona is visited daily by hundreds of tourists who, generally, only have time to see the Nunnery, Abbey and St Oran's Chapel. But for those who have time to make a longer visit, or even spend a night or two on the island, there is much more to see. In the village itself, look out for the Post Office and the Victorian post box. A walk along this street is usually peaceful and the various styles of the cottages, with their pretty gardens across the road, are worth examining. The **Argyll Hotel** stands in a good position along here. Right at the end is **Bishop's House**, which was built in 1893 at the instigation of the then Bishop of Argyll and the Isles. It now belongs to the Church of Scotland and is used as

a retreat and guest house. The atmosphere inside is always welcoming and it is suitable for the disabled. On the right are wonderful views over to Mull.

Instead of taking this right turn as you come off the ferry, you can continue straight ahead up the main road. Leave the Nunnery on your right and follow the road as it goes behind the ruins. On the left is the Primary School and, a little further along is a **memorial to Lord Fraser of Allander**. The buildings set back on the left are the parish church and the manse, both of which are of Thomas Telford's design and were built in 1828. The church is still used as the parish Church of Scotland but the manse is now the **Iona Heritage Centre**. Downstairs are displays about the island's past and present with a small tearoom just around the corner, whilst upstairs is a small flat sometimes used by the minister who comes over from Bunessan.

Continue on the road towards the Abbey and you will pass Maclean's Cross, then the **Columba Hotel** and the **Iona**

bookshop. The latter is well worth spending time in as it has a great selection of interesting books. Beyond the Abbey grounds is the **Iona Community Shop** and, set back, the **Macleod Centre** with the **Iona Pottery and Gallery** on the roadside.

The road now runs peacefully between fields, past the cross commemorating Elizabeth, the first wife of George, Duke of Argyll, and Victoria, their daughter. A short distance beyond this look out for a track to the left which will take you up **Dun I** (*Dun Ee*). This is Iona's highest hill and, though only just over 300ft (91m) high, provides an extensive view on a clear day. From Tiree and Coll, even out to Barra, round past Rum, Eigg and maybe Skye, to Staffa, Ulva and Little Colonsay, to Mull and then Jura and Islay, the panorama is superb. The cairn on top of the hill was built in 1897 for Queen Victoria's Diamond Jubilee. As you look down you will see how sheltered was the site of Columba's original settlement.

On the north side of Dun I is a small pool called '**The Well of Eternal Youth**' where, if a woman bathes her face and hands before sunrise she will become young again! At the foot of the south slope is the remains of the **Hermit's Cell**, which seems to have been set aside for meditation and prayer. Return from here to the road and, in a field below you will see a huge boulder that is thought to have been where the earliest monks had their refectory.

The road continues northwards until you reach a gate beyond which there is a track across to sandy beaches at the end. As there are working farms on Iona you are asked to keep dogs on a lead at all times, especially when crossing open grassland. If you turn left here you will find **Iona Hostel**, which has what must surely be one of the most magnificent views of any Hostel. This end of Iona seems made for peace, tranquillity and contemplation but it was not always so. It is probably up here that the raiders used to land and it might well be that the massacre of many of the monks took place on, or near, the sparkling purity of these serene sands.

Iona

Central Iona

From the ferry there is a road to the south, past the restaurant and general store. Pass the War Memorial and continue along the shoreline to a sharp right turn. The road from here to the other side of the island was built in 1848 to give work to the crofters hard hit by the potato famine. It runs in a straight line to the machair bordering '**The Bay at the Back of the Ocean**', a great sweep of sand where the Atlantic crashes on to the shore in winter, or ripples gently round the rocks on a calm day.

You can either continue your walk by making your way across the moor

Iona Marble Quarry

Many of the 17th- and 18th-century travellers to Mull commented upon the altar table in the ruined Abbey, which seems to have been of fine marble quarried in mediaeval times on Iona. By the 19th century it had been shattered and the fragments scattered. In 1790 George William, the 6th Duke of Argyll, was persuaded to open the Argyll Marble Company but, although quantities of the rock were dug out and sent to Leith and London, the value of the blocks of marble did not cover the expense of removing and transporting them. The quarry was closed and, only four years later, the Marble Company's storehouse, which was in the village, had been converted into a school.

For over 100 years the quarry remained unworked until, in 1907 a firm called Iona Marbles Ltd came into existence. The fashion of the times demanded that all houses should have items of furniture made from, or inlaid with, decorative marble – wash stands, sideboards, occasional tables, coat stands and so on. For a few years this new lease of life lasted, the quarry even obtaining a cutting frame, a gas engine and a derrick, but World War I put paid to the trade.

The quarry again fell silent, this time permanently, but there is still evidence of some of the quarrymen's huts amongst the grass and boulders. Down on the shore are the remains of a tiny powder store, the tanks used to power the engine and the cutting frame. The derrick, which once stood on the quay was swept away in a gale in 1926 but a few rails and a four wheel bogey survive. It must be stressed again, that anyone who penetrates so far must not deface or carry anything away, for Iona Quarry is an important Industrial Archaeological site. It is sufficient to sit and gaze, letting one's imagination recreate the sights and sounds of the quarry in its heyday – the engine, the saw, the blasting, the strenuous activity and the danger which this peaceful spot must once have witnessed.

Golf!

On your way across the flower strewn machair take care not to stumble over a golf pin or put your toe into one of the holes! Golf first came to Iona nearly 120 years ago and, by 1920 the nine-hole course, later extended to 18 holes, became the venue for competitions. There is still the occasional tournament, to raise funds for local charities, on this extremely challenging course!

or coast in the direction of Dun I, up it or round it, and then back to the village along the road past the Abbey, or you can retrace your steps from the golf course, back along the road past the fairy mound on the right, where people used to come on Michaelmas Day to ride round and round it to bring luck. At the cross roads turn left and you will come back to the village via the new **Roman Catholic House of Prayer** and the village hall. The House of Prayer has three single rooms for those of all faiths who want a haven of peace and quiet. It is open all the year.

The south end of Iona

The south end of the island is much less visited than either the north or the middle. It is down here that the island's only fresh water loch is to be found, used as a reservoir for the last 50 years. As you cross the moorland you will notice signs of earlier build-ings and cultivation — some of these are very old, some much more recent. Right at the end is **Columba's Bay** where tradition says that Columba landed. It is even said that his coracle is buried under a grassy mound at the head of the bay but no record of this exists. However, it is the nearest point of the island to Ireland, and there is a hillock with the name 'Cairn with its back to Ireland' nearby, so maybe he did land here.

There are many little bays and caves around the coast at this end of the island. It is hard walking and scrambling and needs care but the rewards are well worth the effort, both for the bays and caves themselves and for the views across the ocean. Even the names of the coves and caves are evocative — Sandeel Bay, Otter Cave, Pigeon's Cave, Port of the False Man, Port of the Big Mouth, Spouting Cave and many more.

At the south eastern tip lies all that remains of **Iona Marble Quarry**. This is a Scheduled Ancient Monument and must be respected and not damaged in any way.

Iona is an island of great beauty, sanctity and mystery. Its setting could hardly be bettered and the surrounding sea sets off this jewel. On wild winter days the Atlantic batters one coast whilst the Sound of Iona froths and seethes with rage, sometimes cutting the island off completely. But on calm summer days the lime green turf and the creamy-white sands are caressed by lazy, lacy fingers of foam from the placid sea. Iona, I, Io, Hy, Hi or Icolumkill, all names used over the centuries, is still a magical place of pilgrimage as it has been for hundreds of years.

The island of Staffa lies about six miles (9.7km) north-east of Iona and four miles (6.4km) south-west of Gometra, off Mull. It is only small – barely a mile long and a quarter of a mile wide – but over the last 200 years it has developed a huge reputation and fascination for visitors. There are several operators who run boat trips in the summer – one from Ulva Ferry and two from Iona and Fionnphort. Landing on Staffa needs care but the boat trip is worth taking for its own sake.

Geology

Staffa has been known about and visited for centuries. Its name probably comes from the Norse word for the staves, which the Vikings used to construct their houses. It is these 'staves' or basalt columns which have given the island its world-wide renown. Geologists believe that Staffa grew gradually as a result of millions of years of volcanic activity in the area. Starting at least 60 million years ago there were repeated immense volcanic eruptions and the resultant lava flows must eventually have been as much as 10,000ft (3048m) thick in places. These great sheets of molten lava contracted and solidified into triangular, quadrangular, pentagonal and hexagonal columns, which were then carved and gouged, stripped and altered by forces of nature. At the same time there was subsidence, uplifting and fault formation, centres of contraction were not regularly spaced and so vertical, horizontal and wavy columns appeared. Over the millennia most of this lava blanket was eroded or dispersed but Staffa and the Treshnish islands remain.

The geological formations of Staffa are awe inspiring. Rising from a base of volcanic debris or tuff are gigantic columns of basalt over 100ft (30.5m) high, with a topping of amorphous basalt like a great frothy frowning green cap. There are no sandy beaches, which makes landing a trifle hazardous on all but the calmest of days. Over the centuries magnificent caves have been formed and it is by one of these, Clamshell Cave, where the safest landing can be found.

Early visitors

Few of the early travellers to the west of Scotland mentioned Staffa except in passing but the fact that its name derives from the Norse must mean that it was known and surely its amazing geology

had been noted. Lying as it does in the Atlantic, it would have been useful strategically for early people, who used the sea and boats as we use roads and cars. Columba's monks might even have gone there as a place of retreat – when they had to abandon Iona in the face of marauders some of the monks went as far as Lake Zurich where they founded two places which they named Stafa and Jona. These are thought to have come from the names of the two islands of Staffa and Iona.

In these days of quick and comfortable travel it is difficult to imagine the hardships faced by early visitors to Staffa. Even getting to Oban would not have been easy and this was only the beginning. Next there was an open boat journey across to Mull which, apart from the dangers and discomforts, was costly. Crossing Mull meant riding a pony over trackless mountains, bogs and rivers for a distance of between ten (16.1km) and 35 miles (56km), depending where the boat had landed. After this came a short boat journey over to Ulva and, finally, a nine-mile (14.5km) row or sail out into the Atlantic. Add to all these perils the primitive inns, the vagaries of the weather and the considerable expense and it is not hard to see why few people ever got to Staffa. It was not until the 1820s when steamboats began regular weekly sailings from Glasgow that people started to arrive in any numbers.

History

However, Staffa had begun its rise from obscurity in 1772. Joseph Banks, then

> ### Legendary formation
>
> A much easier to understand explanation says that a giant called Torquil Macleod lived on the island of Eigg. One day he visited the Giant's Causeway in Ireland. He liked it so much that, secretly, he hacked off a piece that he carried away stuffed into his huge sack. On the way home across the sea his sack burst open and out fell his ill-gotten gains to land with a colossal splash in the Atlantic. There it has lain ever since!

only 29, had been on his way to Iceland and had had his attention drawn to the wonders of this island out in the Atlantic, by a man whom he met by chance. Banks made a detour to see for himself and came back full of excitement, proclaiming that it was one of the greatest natural curiosities in the world. As Banks was a famous naturalist who had been with Captain Cook, his opinion came to the attention of many people who decided it must be worth braving the long and tedious journey to view this remarkable phenomenon.

Banks had found one herdsman on Staffa living a lonely existence. This man seems to have been there still a few years later when the Bishop of London-derry visited the island. During his visit the Bishop was so moved by the poor man's plight that he asked what was his dearest wish to relieve the privations of his loneliness. The herdsman said that he craved a razor and soap so, on his return home the Bishop duly sent a parcel with these items in it!

Famous visitors to Staffa

Sir Walter Scott went twice to Staffa in the early 1800s and wrote about the island in his poem The Lord of the Isles. In 1826 a Yorkshire man was the first to visit Staffa by the new steamboat and, a week later the **Governor of the Bank of France** made the long journey to see this wonder. In 1829, when he was only 20, **Felix Mendelssohn** went by paddle steamer. The weather was bad, everyone was ill and one of his party described Fingal's Cave as a monstrous organ, black, resounding and utterly without purpose! However, in spite of his own sea-sickness, Mendelssohn found that the cave excited him, immediately suggesting a musical phrase in his head. The theme stayed in his musical memory and, twenty years later he composed his Hebridean Overture using it.

By the 1830s there were twice weekly sailings from Oban which usually included an overnight stop each way in Tobermory. More famous people flocked to Staffa. The painter, **JMW Turner**, had an hour there, in bad weather. Subsequently he painted his oil 'Staffa: Fingal's Cave' which was exhibited at the Royal Academy in 1832 provoking mixed reactions because of its indistinctness. **John Keats, Alfred, Lord Tennyson** and **William Wordsworth** all visited the cave, the latter insisting on having time by himself there to absorb the atmosphere and, subsequently, writing four sonnets about the island. **Sir Robert Peel** went in the 1830s and spoke later of having seen 'a temple not made with hands' in which the Atlantic beat 'a note of praise nobler far than any that ever pealed from human organ'. In 1844 The **King of Saxony** took a fifteen-and-a-half-hour day trip from Oban which included a call at Staffa. **Jules Verne** went in 1859 and used Staffa in his novel The Green Ray.

Possibly the greatest boost to the fame of Staffa was the visit of **Queen Victoria, Prince Albert** and their two eldest children in 1847. Queen Victoria wrote in her diary that the appearance of Fingal's Cave was most extraordinary although the effect was splendid, 'like a great entrance to a vaulted hall'. She noticed the shades of the rocks under the water – pink, blue and green. But she did not like the motion of the small boat heaving up and down under her! On the journey to Staffa she did a simple but effective sketch of the Dutchman's Cap, which appears in her diary for August 1847.

By 1800 nine ladies had accompanied their husbands to Staffa. The first to go on her own was Mrs Murray of Kensington. She was a most adventurous traveller and found Staffa so fascinating that she returned two years later. She reported feelings of ecstasy as she gazed at the pillars and domes of the caves and, on entering Fingal's Cave she forgot the world, falling silent with amazement as she felt within her the highest pitch of solemn, pious enthusiasm.

Ownership of Staffa

Since the 1770s Staffa has had relatively few owners. Once the MacQuarries of Ulva had sold it in 1777, it passed to the Campbell family of Auchnaba. Then it went to the MacDonalds of Boisdale before being taken over by trustees who were the Forman family of Edinburgh. It remained in the hands of trustees for 150 years and was then sold to a retired army padre. In 1972 it was bought by Alastair de Watteville. After six years it was briefly in the hands of another owner before passing to a business man who, in 1986, wishing to commemorate his wife's 60th birthday, gave Staffa to the National Trust for Scotland. Over the years many improvements have been made to the landing facilities for visitors and now there is a steel and concrete jetty and stairway up the cliffs at Clamshell Cave.

Visiting the island

The usual landing place is beside the Clamshell Cave. One side of the entrance is formed from curving bent columns, which give the cave its name as they form the ribs of a boat or a scallop shape. The cave is about 30ft (9m) high, only 16ft (4.9m) wide but its length is 130ft (40m). Having scrambled off the boat here you can either climb up the stairs to the flat grassy top of the island or pick your way carefully along the causeway towards **Fingal's Cave**. The causeway is formed from the tops of small or broken columns making a tessellated pavement like stepping stones. It is about 300yd (274m) long and on the left is the islet called **The Herdsman** which looks like a large pimply rubber ball. Look out for **Fingal's Wishing Chair** in the cliff on the right. If you sit in this natural formation and wish, it will come true. Go round the bending columns and you will reach the cave.

Fingal's cave is the most famous feature of the island and the best overall view is from a boat. From the sea it looks like a yawning whale's mouth,

a masterpiece carved and chiselled by nature, a Gothic cathedral wrought by man – the descriptions have been varied and endless. Undoubtedly it is breathtakingly impressive. From the narrow causeway inside the cave its awesome size can begin to be appreciated. It is 65ft (20m) high, 50ft (15m) wide and 230ft (70m) deep.

On a calm day the light reflects off the quivering water, glistens on the rocks and rainbows sparkle in the semi-darkness. The rhythmic suck and swell of the sea near the mouth of the cave becomes deeper and more eerie towards the mysterious darkness at the back. Behind, in the distance are the cries of the sea birds and, through the perfectly arched entrance, Iona floats on the serenely shining sea. The solemnity, reminiscent of a cathedral, induces a meditative mood as the water sighs and susurrates, breathing gently and deeply around you.

To the west of Fingal's cave are the sheer cliffs known as the Great Face. These average over 50ft (15m) with the highest point being over 100ft (30m) and are almost impossible to appreciate fully except from the sea.

Other caves

Just beyond the Great Face is the **Boat Cave**, only 14ft (4.3m) high, 12ft (3.7m) wide and 150ft (46m) deep. Round the south western tip of Staffa is **MacKinnon's cave**. This faces the full force of the Atlantic and is often a turmoil of sea and spray. Its surroundings are white with the droppings of hundreds of sea birds which wheel and cry, or cling to tiny ledges, crammed close together. The cave is 50ft (15m) high, 48ft (14.6m) wide and a remarkable 224ft (68m) long. It seems to have been named after Abbot MacKinnon, the last Abbot of Iona who died around 1500. **Cormorant cave** is tucked in a little way north of MacKinnon's cave and is smaller but at the back it has a dark, winding, narrow tunnel which communicates with MacKinnon's Cave.

If you scramble up to the top of the island you will find that it is flat and fertile. From the summit, which is only 135ft (41m) high, there is a 360 view of great grandeur. Early visitors had found as many as 16 people living here in two small huts. Between them, it was reported, they had eight cows, one bull, twelve sheep, two horses, one pig, two dogs, one cock and eight hens – imagine ferrying all those across in a small open boat! They grew mostly barley, oats and potatoes. The population declined and the island came to be used only occasionally for grazing a few beasts. Around 1816 the then owner, Ranald MacDonald, started to build a more substantial dwelling, perhaps with an eye to the increasing number of visitors! But this was never finished and the last of the ruins disappeared during the 1930s.

The name 'Fingal'

The origin of the name is wrapped in myth and, of course, there are several versions. Some say that Finn MacCool was an Irish giant who built both the Giant's Causeway and Fingal's cave. Another legend relates that a nine headed monster once lived in the cave.

Music in Fingal's Cave

As well as Mendelssohn hearing the theme of his *Hebrides Overture* in the sound of the sea, there have been at least three other musical episodes in the cave. In 1815 a Dr Sandy Campbell heard the bagpipes being played in there. He described its resounding tones, combined with the thunder of the waves, as sublime. Then, in 1897 a large group of eminent churchmen, who had been on Iona to celebrate the 1300th anniversary of Columba's death, were taken to the cave. Once inside they sang the 103rd psalm together, which must have made an awesome sound.

Fingal's Cave

Finally, in September 2001 Scottish Natural Heritage and the National Trust for Scotland invited the people of Mull and Iona to Staffa to celebrate its declaration as a National Nature Reserve, an honour given to only the best of Scotland's nature sites. Once there, the 'Mendelssohn on Mull' wind ensemble would play the *Hebrides Overture.* On the day there was a force 9 wind but the musicians, in bow ties and dinner jackets, plus their instruments and music stands and their intrepid audience, battled their way to the cave. In the words of one of this audience: 'To listen to the *Hebrides Overture* being played in Fingal's cave in a gale is bizarre to say the least but all thoughts of seasickness were dispelled by the magic of the moment.' The oldest person there was 85 and the youngest was 5 months.

He kept his captives until he had nine and then consumed them all at once. Or perhaps you prefer the version that tells us that a giant called Fingal, with his wife and family, lived in the cave. It is said that his ghost may still be seen drifting about the island like a huge white bird. Finally, it is thought that in the third century there was an Irish general called Finn MacCunhail who was similar to King Arthur in that he had a group of knights around him. Stories of their heroic deeds would have come to Scotland as the Gaels moved across the sea and a corruption of his name might have been chosen for this wondrous cave.

Natural environment

One of the delights of Staffa is its bird and plant life. Puffins are a great joy to watch especially when, as here, they are so tame. They will land at your feet with bills full of food for their young and will tell you to move your feet if you happen to be standing in or near their burrow. Their attempts to get airborne are fun to watch but they only come to land for a few months in the year to lay and hatch their eggs. By the end of August they will have returned to sea where they spend the rest of the year.

Cormorants and shags abound and are often to be seen standing on a rock with their wings half open as they hang them out to dry. Black-headed gulls and fulmars, razorbills, guillemots and kittiwakes can also be seen by the score. Off shore there are seals in plenty, sometimes an otter, dolphin, porpoise or even a whale. As many as 150 species of plants have been found on the island, an unusually great number for so small a place. This is partly due to its variety of soil types and the lack of bracken or heather.

Staffa has been called an island of latent power – grand and strong. It needs to be painted in oils with the deep hues of umber, ochre, sepia and sienna for the cliffs, topped by viridian and hookers greens, with ultramarine, Prussian blue, ivory and black seas. Seen from a distance on bad days, the welter of foam and spray as the sea snarls and lashes the towering colonnades will never be forgotten. Neither will a calm summer sunset, if you can be there at the right time. As the sun sinks the sky gradually turns a translucent green shot with saffron whilst luminous rays of opalescent light shimmer across the water and the silhouettes of the Treshnish Islands become violet, then black as the glowing, triumphant ball sinks with an almost audible hiss. You might even see the split second flash of the 'green ray' which Jules Verne described in his novel. If you do, it will give you the power to see through falsehood and deception wherever you go. Just one more aspect of the magic that is Staffa.

Local stamps

In 1968 a local boatman started to sell Staffa stamps to his visitors. These proved a popular attraction and, six years later, the owner of the island commissioned new sets of stamps which could be bought on board the boats, posted in a box installed at Clamshell Cave, franked on the return voyage and handed in to a post office on Mull. This arrangement lasted until 1978 when it was withdrawn. Philatelists might like to keep a look out for Staffa stamps.

Travelling to Mull

Traveline
☎ 0871 200 22 33
for general information www.traveline.org.uk

Scottish Citylink coaches
☎ 08705 505050
www.citylink.co.uk

Scotrail Services
☎ 08457 5500 33
www.scotrail.co.uk

Caledonian MacBrayne Ltd
Ferry Terminal, Gourock, PA19 1QP
General enquiries and car reservations:
☎ 01475 650100 Fax 01475 637607
Booking Hotline ☎ 08000 66 5000 freephone
www.calmac.co.uk

Calmac Head Office, Gourock
General enquiries: ☎ 01475 650100
Service information line ☎ 08000 5400 freephone
www.calmac.co.uk

Car reservations:

Oban Office
☎ 01631 566688
Fax: 01631 566588
Craignure Office
☎ 01680 812343 Fax: 01680 812433

Fishnish–Lochaline
☎ 01680 812343 Fax: 01688 302660 or
01688 302017

Tobermory–Kilchoan
☎ 01688 302017 or 01680 812343
www.calmac.co.uk

Disabled passengers
For help on railways ☎ 08456 057021
for help on piers or ferries ☎ 01631 566688

Ferry to Ulva
(foot passengers and cycles only)
☎ D Munro 0791 9902407 or 01688 500241
(privately operated)
www.ulva.mull.com

Ferry to Iona
(foot passengers, cycles and authorised vehicles only)
☎ 01680 812343
www.calmac.co.uk
Disabled passengers OK

For general advice on travelling and accommodation:
Tourist Information Centre
Craignure, Mull, PA65 6AY
☎ 01680 812377 / 08707 200610
E-mail: info@mull.visitscotland.com
Open: April-October

Tobermory, Mull
E-mail: info@tobermory.visitscotland.com
☎ 08707 200625

Accommodation
There are many hotels, guest houses, bed and breakfasts and self-catering units on Mull and Iona. Full details can be obtained from the Tourist Office in Craignure.
The Youth Hostel is in Tobermory ☎/Fax 01688 302481 and there is a hostel on Iona ☎ 01681 700781
E-mail: info@ionahostel.co.uk www.ionahostel.co.uk
Camping/caravan sites can be found near Tobermory ☎ 01688 302624, Calgary Bay, Craignure ☎01680 812496, Balemeanach ☎ 01680 300342, Killiechronan, Fidden and Fionnphort ☎01681 700213.

Air Field
For information about this ☎ 01680 300402

Banks

Clydesdale

Main Street, Tobermory, PA75 6NY ☎ 0845
7826818 Fax: 01688 302505 (Cash point also)

Royal Bank of Scotland

26 George Street, PA34 5SA Oban
☎ 01631 563639

Bank of Scotland

Station Road, Oban PA34 4LL ☎ 01631 563639.

All three banks have mobile vans that tour around
Mull. Ask in POs for times and stopping places.
Bureaux de change: Clydesdale Bank, Tobermory
☎ 08457 826818; The Ferry Shop, Fionnphort
☎ 01681 700470; TIC, Craignure ☎01680 812377;
TIC, Tobermory ☎ 01688 302182.

Boat hire/fishing/whale watching/diving/ inter-island cruises/wildlife expeditions

There are many of these – the list below is only a selection.
Tourist Offices will be able to help you and also the Mull and Iona ranger Service. ☎ 01680 300640,
E-mail: jdunlop@mict.co.uk

Sealife surveys

Ledaig, Tobermory
☎ 01688 302916
www.sealifesurveys.com

Silverswift

Raraig House, Raeric Rd, Tobermory
☎ 01688 302390
www.tobermoryboatcharters.co.uk

Alternative Boat Hire

Iona & Fionnphort
☎ 01681 700537
www.boattripsiona.com

MV Amidas

book via Tackle and Books, Main Street,
Tobermory
☎ 01688 302336
www.mv-amidas.co.uk

Hebridean Whale and Dolphin Trust

Main Street, Tobermory
☎ 01688 302620
email: hwdt@sol.co.uk
or info@sealifesurveys.com

Hebridean Adventure

Sailing ship trips
Tobermory
☎ 01688 302017
www.hebrideanadventure.co.uk

Discover Mull

Dervaig
☎ 01688 400415 or 07780600367
www.discovermull.co.uk

MV Volante

Fionnphort,
Iona
☎ 01681 700362
www.volanteiona.com

Wildlife Expeditions

David Woodhouse
Ulva Ferry
☎ 01688 500121
www.scotlandwildlife.com

Pam & Arthur Brown

Dervaig
☎ 01688 400415 or 07780600367
E-mail: enquiries@discovermull.co.uk

Richard Atkinson

Island Encounters
Salen ☎ 01680 300441
www.mullwildlife.co.uk
Wings Over Mull (bird sanctuary) Craignure
☎ 01680 812594

Explore Mull Wildlife

Dervaig
☎ 01688 400209
View sea eagles from a hide (May, June and July)
☎ 01631 566155

Angling

Benmore Estate ☎ 01680 300229
Pennyghael Estate ☎ 01681 704232
Tobermory Angling Association ☎ 01688 302447

Treshnish Islands and Staffa

From Iona and Fionnphort – Kirkpatrick ☎ 01681 700358
E-mail: dk@staffatrips.f9.co.uk www.staffatrips.f9.co.uk;
Grant Tours ☎ 01681 700338
www.staffatours.com
From Ulva Ferry, Oban – Turus Mara ☎ 01688 400242/297 or 01631 566999
E-mail: info@turusmara.com www.turusmara.com
From Oban/Craignure by Bowman's Coaches ☎ 01631 563221
www.bowmanstours

Books

The following is a small selection of many which can be obtained from Tourist Offices and bookshops on Mull and Iona, and in Oban. All, except the first five, have been selected because they are small paperback books.

Mull: the island and its people
Jo Currie. Birlinn, Edinburgh

The Isle of Mull
PA Macnab. David and Charles

Staffa
Donald B MacCulloch. David and Charles

Argyll Volume 3
Royal Commission on Ancient and Historical Monuments. HMSO

Iona
E Mairi MacArthur. Colin Baxter Photography, Grantown-on-Spey.

Ardmeanach: a hidden corner of Mull
J LeMay. The New Iona Press.

Birds of Mull
M Madders and P Snow. Saker Press

Glen More
J LeMay and J Gardner. Brown and Whittaker, Tobermory

Historic Visitors to Mull, Iona & Staffa
Eve Eckstein. Excalibur Press, London

Kilmore Church, Dervaig
Hilary M. Peel. Nevis Press

Mull Family Names
J Currie. Brown and Whittaker, Tobermory

Mull in the Making
Rosalind Jones. Rosalind Jones, Mull

Mull: Natural History
J Whittaker. Brown and Whittaker, Tobermory

Salen Church
Hilary M Peel. CCC Designs, Ulva Ferry, Mull

The Place Names of Mull
Duncan M MacQuarrie. John G Eccles, Inverness

Walking in North Mull
O Brown and J Whittaker. Brown and Whittaker, 8th ed.

Walking in South Mull
O Brown and J Whittaker. Brown and Whittaker, 2001 ed.

The Isle of Ulva
J Howard and A Jones. Harlequin Press, Oban

Iona: a guide to the Monuments
Royal Commission on Ancient & Historical Monuments. HMSO

Staffa
Alastair de Watteville. Romsey Fine Art

Churches

Church of Scotland
Tobermory/Salen ☎ 01688 302356
Bunessan ☎ 01681 700227

Episcopal Church, Gruline
☎ 01680 300601

Roman Catholic Church, Tobermory
☎ 01688 302317

Evangelical Church, Tobermory
☎ 01680 300536

Baptist church, Bunessan
☎ 01681 700398

RC House of Prayer, Iona
☎ 01681 700369

Bishops House, Iona
☎ 01681 700800
email: bhiona@argyll.anglican.org

Iona Abbey
☎ 01681 700404

Iona Macleod Centre
☎ 01681 700404

Findhorn, Erraid Island
☎ 01681 700384

Diving

R. Barlow, Tobermory ☎ 01688 302147
Pegasus Diving, Tobermory ☎ 01688 302112
Seamore Diving, Fionnphort ☎ 01681 700462

Emergencies

☎ 999 or the following:

Police
Tobermory ☎ 01688 302016
Salen ☎ 01680 300322
Craignure ☎ 01680 812322
Bunessan ☎ 01681 700222
Oban ☎ 01631 562213

Fire
☎ 999

Coastguard
☎ 999 or ☎ 01688 302200

Lifeboat
Tobermory ☎ 01688 302143 or 07768556107

Events

March	Mull Drama Festival
April	Mull Music Festival
May	Rugby Sevens with teams from all over Scotland
June	Mendelssohn on Mull Festival
July	Round Mull Yacht race
	Highland Games, Tobermory
	West Highland Yacht Week
August	Mull and Morvern Agricultural Show, Salen Bunessan Agricultural Show
September	Isle of Mull Mod (Scotland's equivalent to Wales' Eisteddfod)
	Taste of Mull and Iona Food Festival
October	Tour of Mull Car Rally

An Tobar in Tobermory, has a year round programme for all ages - music, art exhibitions, concerts, workshops and talks.

Iona Abbey, the Macleod Centre and Camas all provide environmental activities, outdoor pursuits and creative arts and craft courses from April to October.

During the summer there are art exhibitions, flower and vegetable shows, regattas, fishing competitions, ceilidhs, dances and meetings of clubs and societies to which visitors are welcome. Look in the local papers, or shop windows, for details.

Fishing

For information contact Tackle and Books, Tobermory: ☎ 01688 302336 or Browns, Tobermory: ☎ 01688 302020 where you will get details of fishing on the Mishnish and Aros Lochs, Loch Ba and the river Ba, Loch Assapol, the river Caldoir, Loch Uisg and the Lochdon estuary, as well as sea angling.

Food, Drink & Crafts

Ardalanish Organic Farm & Weaving Mill, Ross of Mull
☎ 01681 700265
info@ardalanishfarm.co.uk www.isleofmullweavers.co.uk
Organic beef, mutton, vegetables, tweed, scarves

Brown & Son, Tobermory
☎ 01688 302020
www.brownstobermory.aol.uk

Tobermory and Iona malt whisky
Co-op, Main Street, Tobermory
☎ 01688 302004
Tobermory beers

Island Bakery
Main Street, Tobermory
☎ 01688 302225
E-mail: deli@islandbakery.co.uk
Local bread, delicatessen & biscuits

Mull Butcher's Shop
Main Street, Tobermory
☎ 01688 302021
E-mail: mullbutchers@mict.co.uk
Fresh vacuum packed local beef, lamb, pork & venison

Isle Of Mull Cheese
Sgriob-ruadh Farm Dairy, by Tobermory
☎ 01688 302235
www.isleofmullcheese.co.uk
Award winning local cheeses

Tobermory Fish Company
Baliscate, Tobermory
☎ 01688 302120
E-mail: sales@tobermoryfish.co
Local grown and smoked trout, mussels, salmon & scallops

Mull Organic Mushrooms
Dervaig
☎ 01688 400433
E-mail: mushrooms@jjaustin.idps.co.uk
Organic shiitake

Isle of Mull Oysters
Penmore, Dervaig
☎ 01688 400268 or 01688 400312

I & H Mackay
Lagganulva, Ulva Ferry
☎ 01688 500139
E-mail: lagganulva@gmail.com
Local beef, lamb & mutton

Ardmore Fish
Salen
☎ 01680 300468 or 0777 4214552

Isle of Mull Chutney
Lochdon
☎ 01680 812402
E-mail: Psmall502@aol.com
Handmade chutney, pickles and preserves from local produce

Inverlussa Mussel Farm
by Lochdon
☎ 01680 812436

The Ferry Shop
Fionnphort
☎ 01681 700470
E-mail: bruntonmull@aol.com
Local bread, meat, fish, vegetables & eggs

Ulva Oysters
Ulva
☎ 01688 500264

Garages

Craignure
Bayview ☎ 01680 812444 (plus petrol)

Dervaig
☎ 01688 400325

Fionnphort
MacDougall, ☎ 01688 700294
Night ☎ 01688 700271 (plus petrol)

Salen
Kennedy ☎ 01680 300396

Tobermory
MacKay ☎ 01688 302103
Night ☎ 01688 302304 (plus petrol)
Petrol

See garages and also:
Craignure: 01680812301
Salen: 01680300326
Tobermory: 01688302154

NOTE: There is no petrol in Bunessan but there are two places 2 miles or so beyond. Remember it is over 30 miles from Craignure, over 40 miles from Salen and over 60 miles from Tobermory, via Ulva Ferry, to these petrol pumps!

Getting around

ALWAYS STOP ON THE LEFT HAND SIDE OF THE ROAD, EITHER IN OR OPPOSITE A PASSING PLACE, TO LET OTHERS PASS OR OVERTAKE

Approximate driving times

When on Mull, mileages have less relevance to the time of a journey because of the nature of the roads which are mostly single track. The following times are, of course, only approximate as much will depend on the time of day, who is on the roads and how often you stop to admire the view or wildlife!

Tobermory to Salen 30 mins 10 miles (16km)
Salen to Craignure 15 mins 10 miles (16km)
Craignure to Bunessan 45 mins 30 miles (48km)
Bunessan to Fionnphort 15 mins 5 miles (8km)
Tobermory to Dervaig 15 mins 5 miles (8km)
Dervaig to Ulva Ferry, via Calgary 30 mins 15 miles (24km) steep hills
Ulva Ferry to Salen 20 mins 7 miles (4.4km)
Salen to Bunessan, via the Gribun rocks 70 mins 35 miles (56km)

Public Transport

The free Argyll and Bute Area Transport Guide gives much information about getting around Mull without a car. It can be obtained from the local Tourist Offices and in Oban.

Buses

Tobermory – Salen – Craignure and Craignure – Bunessan – Fionnphort routes are operated by:

Bowman's Coaches

www.bowmanstours.co.uk
☎ 01680 812313 or 01631 563221

Tobermory – Dervaig – Calgary is operated by:

RN Carmichael

☎ 01688 302220

Taxis

Tobermory: ☎ 0781 0666222; for 8 people 01688 302204; 07760 426 351
Bunessan ☎ 01681700507 or 0788 7774550 8 seats
Fionnphort ☎ 01681 700294 or 0785 0630061 8 seats
Iona ☎ 0781 0325990

Car hire

Bayview Garage
Craignure (16 seater minibus also)
☎ 01680 812444

Mull Car hire
Glenforsa
☎ 01680 300402

Mackay's Garage
Tobermory
☎ 01688 302103

MacDougall's Garage
Fionnphort (8 seater minibus also)
☎ 01681 700294

Cycle hire

Tobermory, Brown's ☎ 01688 302020
Fionnphort ☎ 01681 700470
Salen ☎ 01680 300501

Craignure ☎ 01680 812496
Iona ☎ 01681 700357

Golf

Tobermory
contact Browns in Tobermory, Main Street ☎ 01688 302020
Craignure ☎ 01680 300402

Local Papers

There are two local papers which are published monthly *Am Muileach* and *Round and About*.

Maps

OS Landranger Series Nos. 47, 48 and 49. Scale 1:50,000 (2cm to 1km or 1.25in to 1 mile)
OS Explorer Series Nos. 373, 374 and 375. Scale 1:25,000 (4cm to 1km or 2.5in to 1 mile)
OS Leisure map of Iona and Mull, Scale for Iona 1:10,000 and for Mull 1:115,000
Nicolson Tourist Map of Oban and Mull. Scale 1in to 1.6 miles.

Medical Information

Bunessan doctor
☎ 01681 700261

Salen doctor
☎ 01680 300327

Tobermory doctor
☎ 01688 302013

Dentist
☎ 01688 302105

Dunaros Hospital, Salen
☎ 01680 300392

Chemist, Tobermory
☎ 01688 302431

Photography

workshops/courses

Phil McDermott Photography
www.philmcdermott.com/mull-photography-workshops/
☎ 01680 812187

Pony trekking

Killiechronan area
☎ 01680 300313 / 0774 8807 447

Post Offices

Aros (Salen)
☎ 01680 300321

Lochbuie
☎0168 0814225

Iona
☎ 01681 700515

Bunessan
☎ 01681 700252

Lochdon
☎ 01680 812325

Craignure
☎ 01680 812301

Pennyghael
☎ 01681 704229

Dervaig
☎ 01688 400208

Tobermory
☎ 01688 302058

Fionnphort
☎ 01681 700470

Ulva Ferry
☎ 01688 500245

Tourist Information Offices and sites online

Craignure, The Pier
☎ 08707 200610
email: info@mull.visitscotland.com

Tobermory, The Pier
☎ 08707 200625 (April to October)

Oban
☎ 08707 200 630

Kilchoan
☎ 01972 510222 April to October + limited winter opening)

Holiday Mull
www.holidaymull.org.uk
email: holidaymull@ukonline.co.uk

Mull & Iona Community Trust
www.mict.co.uk

Veterinary surgeon

Fishnish, between Salen and Craignure
☎ 01680 300319

Visitor Attractions and Wet Weather Activities

Hebridean Whale and Dolphin Trust, Tobermory, PA75 6NU	☎ 01688 302620	page 19
Museum, Tobermory, PA75 6NY	☎ 01688 302493	page 20
Whisky Distillery, PA75 6NR	☎ 01688 302647	page 24
Balamory houses, PA75 6PB		page 22
An Tobar Exhibitions, Argyl Terrace, Tobermory PA75 6PB	☎ 01688 302211	page 21
Children's Farm	☎ 01688 302941	page 22
Sgriob-ruadh Farm	☎ 01688 302235	page 25
Tobermory Golf Course		page 25
The Old Byre Heritage Centre, Dervaig	☎ 01688 400229	page 29
Pony Trekking, Killiechronan	☎ 0774 8807 447	page 36
Craignure Golf Course		page 41
Swimming Pool		page 43
Narrow Gauge Railway	☎ 01680 812494	page 43
Torosay Castle & Gardens, Craignure PA65 6AY	☎ 01680 812421	page 44
Duart Castle, Craignure, PA64 6AP	☎ 01680 812309	page 44
Ardalanish Organic Farm	☎ 01681 700265	page 61
Ross of Mull Historical Centre, Bunessan	☎ 01681 700659	page 61
Columba Centre, Fionnphort		page 62
Ulva Heritage Centre, Ulva Ferry	☎ 01688 500241	page 65
Iona Abbey	☎ 01681 700404	page 74
Iona Heritage Centre	☎ 01681 700576	page 78

Index

A

Alfred, Lord Tennyson 84
An Sean Dun 27
An Tobar an Arts Centre & Gallery 21
Archaeology 9
Ardmeanach 52
Ardmore Point 28
Argyll Hotel 78
Argyll Terrace 22
Aros 36
Aros Castle 36
Aros House 22
Aros Park 23
Asknish Bay 14

B

Bac Beag 68
Bac Mor 68
Balamory 22
Balemeanach 53
Baliscate 23
Balmeanach Park 41
Ben More 54
Ben Talaidh 41
Bloody Bay 28
Brolas 58
Bunessan 61

C

Calgary 29
Calgary Bay 30
Calgary Castle 30
Calve Island 22
Carsaig 58
Carthouse Gallery 29
Chapel of Kilmore 28
Church of Scotland 39
clan wars 10
Coladoir River 51, 55
Columba Centre 62
Crackaig 32
Craignure 41
Croggan 49
Croggan pie 49
Croig 29

D

Daisy Cheape 53
Dervaig 28
Duart 44
Duart Castle 43
Dun Aisgain 32
Dun Ara 27
Dun Ara castle 27
Dutchman's Cap 68

E

Eas Fors Waterfall 35
Erraid 68
Erray Farm House 25

F

Felix Mendelsohn 84
Fidden 62
Fingal's Cave 85,86
Fionnphort 61
Fishnish 6
Fishnish ferry 41

G

Geology 8
Glass Barn 25
Glenforsa 42
Glengorm 25
Glengorm Castle 25
Glen More 50
Glenmore 48
Gometra 32, 63
Gorrie's Leap 60
Governor of the Bank
of France 84
Grasspoint 45
Gribun 31, 53
griobruadh Farm 25
Gruline 57
Gualan Dhubh 36
Guillemots 63

H

Hadrian's wall 8
Haun 32
History 10
HMS Dartmouth 16

I

Inch Kenneth 65
Inniemore Lodge-Studios 58
Iona 70
Iona Abbey 74
Iona Marble Quarry 80
Iona Pottery and Gallery 79
island of Erraid 62

J

JMW Turner 84
John Keats 84
Jules Verne 84

K

Kelp 69
Kilchoan 6
Kilmore Church 26
Kilninian church 33
Kilvickeon 60
King of Saxony 84
Kinloch 58
Kintra 62

L

Lochaline 6
Loch Assapol 15,60
Loch Ba 55
Lochbuie 47
Loch Cuin 29
Lochdonhead 45
Loch na Keal 34,36
Loch Scridain 51,58
Loch Spelve 45
Loch Tuath 32
Loch Uisg 45
Lord Fraser of Allander 78
Lord Ullin 34

M

Mackinnon's cave 53
Macquarie's Mausoleum 57
Malcolm's Point, 60

Marine Archaeology 16
Mishnish 28
Mishrush Lochs 26
Mitford sisters 66
Morvern 6
Moy Castle 47
Mull 6
Mull and Iona Museum 20
Mull Combination Poorhouse 28
Mull Pottery 23

N

Newdale 28

O

Oban 6
Old Byre Heritage Centre 29
Ormaig 65

P

Pedlar's Grave 56
Prince Albert 84

Q

Queen Victoria 84

R

Reudle school 32
Rhuba-nan-Gall 27
Ross 58
Ross of Mull Historical Centre 61
Rubha-nan-Gall 25

S

Salen 39
Scallastle bay 41
Scoor 60
Shiaba 60
Sir Robert Peel 84
Sorne Point 27
Spanish treasure 21
Sput Dubh 23
Staffa 14, 82
St Mary's Well 23
Stone Circle 46
Sunipol 29

T

The Well of Eternal Youth 79
Thomas Telford 39
Tireragan 62
Tobermory 18
Tobermory cemetery 23
Tobermory Distillery 24
Tobermory golf course 25
Torloisk 33
Torosay 44
Treshnish Islands 32, 67

U

Ulva 32,63

W

Western Isles Hotel 20
William Wordsworth 84
World War II 21